WITHIN THESE PRISON WALLS

LORENZO SNOW'S
RECORD BOOK, 1886–1897

WITHIN THESE PRISON WALLS

LORENZO SNOW'S
RECORD BOOK, 1886–1897

Edited by
Andrew H. Hedges and Richard Neitzel Holzapfel

RELIGIOUS STUDIES CENTER
BRIGHAM YOUNG UNIVERSITY

DESERET
BOOK

Published by the Religious Studies Center, Brigham Young University, Provo, Utah, in cooperation with Deseret Book Company, Salt Lake City, Utah.
http://rsc.byu.edu/

Printed in the United States of America by Sheridan Books Inc.

Jacket design by Nathan Richardson. Photos courtesy of Church History Library.
Interior design by Jonathon Owen.

Library of Congress Cataloging-in-Publication Data

Snow, Lorenzo, 1814–1901.
Within these prison walls: Lorenzo Snow's record book, 1886–1897 / edited by Andrew H. Hedges and Richard Neitzel Holzapfel.
    p. cm.
Includes bibliographical references and index.
    ISBN 978-0-8425-2762-0 (hard cover : alk. paper)
    1. Snow, Lorenzo, 1814–1901—Diaries. 2. Snow, Lorenzo, 1814–1901—Imprisonment. 3. Polygamy—Religious aspects—Church of Jesus Christ of Latter-day Saints—History—19th century. 4. Church of Jesus Christ of Latter-day Saints—Doctrines—History—19th century. I. Hedges, Andrew H., 1966- II. Holzapfel, Richard Neitzel. III. Title. IV. Series.

BX8695 .S75A3 2010
289.3092—dc22

                    2010015799

For my mother and father, Ann and Ward Hedges.
                    —Andrew Hedges

For Stephen H. Smoot, missionary companion par excellence, friend, and supporter.
                    —Richard Neitzel Holzapfel

CONTENTS

Lorenzo Snow's Record Book Entries

Acknowledgments

All projects such as this one are completed with the help of many hands. First and foremost, we are grateful for Brent Ashworth's willingness to share items from his important and significant Mormon Americana collection. Lorenzo Snow's record book is one of many items he has allowed us to use over the years. His support and interest in preserving the past is very much appreciated. A copy of the record book, "Snow, Lorenzo, 1814–1901. Notebook, 1886–1897," is found at the Church History Library, The Church of Jesus Christ of Latter-day Saints, in Salt Lake City.

We appreciate the efforts of Brett G. Scharffs, Francis R. Kirkham Professor of Law at the J. Reuben Clark Law School and associate director of the International Center of Law and Religion Studies, Brigham Young University, in helping us contextualize the legal issues involved in Lorenzo Snow's judicial odyssey.

Additionally we are grateful to Nathan B. Oman, an assistant professor at the Marshall-Wythe School of Law at the College of William & Mary and visiting professor at Cornell Law School, for his insights and clarification of legal aspects surrounding the Mormons and the antipolygamy crusade.

We acknowledge the help of Thomas G. Alexander, former Lemuel Hardison Redd Jr. Professor of Western American History at Brigham Young University, who read the introduction and provided important insights and suggestions that improved the telling of this important story.

We are also grateful for the assistance of staff members at the Church History Library. Specifically, we appreciate the help of Christy Best, William W. Slaughter, and April Williamson. Larry Draper and Russell C. Taylor of the L. Tom Perry Special Collections, Harold B. Lee Library, Brigham Young University, in Provo also handled special requests.

We wish to thank the BYU Religious Studies (RSC) staff, R. Devan Jensen, Brent R. Nordgren, and Joany O. Pinegar, for their important contributions to this project. Additionally, we appreciate the help of the student editing and design team at the RSC: Caitlin S. Channer, Jacob F. Frandsen, James D. Jensen, Kate Lindsay, Jonathon R. Owen, Rosalind E. Ricks, and Dayna K. Thomas.

Additionally, we thank Kip Sperry, a colleague from the Department of Church History and Doctrine, for his family history research that helped us understand Lorenzo Snow's family relationships.

We also appreciate the efforts of our student research assistants, Andrew M. Bateman, Christopher J. Keneipp, Laurie R. Mildenhall, LeAnn Paulsen, and Benjamin H. Tingey. In particular, we would like to thank Kipp Muir, another student research assistant, who took most of the responsibility in helping us get this project completed during the past year.

Finally, we also wish to thank two students, Robert F. Schwartz and Laura Morrison, who began working on this project many years ago. Robert laid an important groundwork for this project, and Laura completed the initial research for the biographical register.

INTRODUCTION

ROM the earliest times, men and women have suffered imprisonment and banishment for their religious convictions. There
are numerous examples in the Old Testament and during the
intertestamental period, including Jeremiah and Daniel. Jesus Christ
and John the Baptist are perhaps some of the best-known examples
of those who experienced persecution from powerful institutions.

In the Sermon on the Mount, Jesus told the disciples, "Blessed are
they which are persecuted for righteousness' sake: for theirs is the
kingdom of heaven. Blessed are ye, when men shall revile you, and
persecute you, and shall say all manner of evil against you falsely, for
my sake. Rejoice, and be exceeding glad: for great is your reward in
heaven: for so persecuted they the prophets which were before you"
(Matthew 5:10–12). Jesus knew that this would not change—people
of conviction would often find themselves in conflict with political
regimes and religious opponents.

Later, the resurrected Christ specifically challenged the Saints
to remain faithful even in the face of imprisonment and death:
"Fear none of those things which thou shalt suffer: behold, the devil
shall cast some of you into prison, that ye may be tried; and ye shall
have tribulation ten days: be thou faithful unto death, and I will
give thee a crown of life" (Revelation 2:10). Trials and tribulations
are not only to be expected, they are promised.

In the decades following Jesus' Ascension, the book of Acts chronicles the arrest and imprisonment of the disciples, including Church leaders such as Peter and James. In some cases they were miraculously delivered (see Acts 5:18–19; 12:4–17; 16:22–40), but at other times they were not (see Acts 12:1–2). Ironically, one of those who arrested the Saints and threw them into prison was eventually incarcerated for the very cause he once fought. Paul's early career as a persecutor changed when he met the risen Lord on the road to Damascus (see Acts 9:1–9). As one of Christ's witnesses, he was later imprisoned on a number of occasions (see 2 Corinthians 11:23).

PRISON AND EXILE WRITINGS

Paul is well known not only as an important missionary, establishing churches in Asia (modern Turkey), Macedonia, and Achaia (modern Greece), but also for his extensive letter-writing career. As many as five of Paul's New Testament letters may have been written while he was incarcerated. Known today as the prison letters, they include Ephesians, Philippians, Colossians, Philemon, and 2 Timothy. In one of these letters, the Apostle introduced himself as "Paul, a prisoner of Jesus Christ" (Philemon 1:1). These prison letters have provided Christians then and now with an example of steadfastness, insights into the human dilemma, and encouragement and hope during times of overwhelming adversity.

In addition to Paul's letters written during confinement, the New Testament contains another important letter that might be considered prison writing. John's circular letter to the seven churches in Asia is found in the book of Revelation. For nearly two thousand years, Christians have widely believed that John wrote the letter while he was a prisoner "for the word of God, and for the testimony of Jesus Christ" (Revelation 1:9). Today, some scholars suggest John was banished to Patmos rather than imprisoned there; either way, however, he was effectively a prisoner for his beliefs.

Since Paul's and John's day, prison writings have become an important, although often underappreciated, genre of Christian literature. Sociologist Ioan Davies opined, "Much of the influential literature of Judeo-Christian civilization was composed under conditions of incarceration or involuntary exile." He added, "It is arguable that it is impossible to understand [Western] thought without recognizing the central significance of prison and banishment in its theoretical and literary composition."[1] Surprisingly, thousands of prison writings have been published, some of which are rather well known today.[2] Among the most widely read prison writings are the letters of Sir Thomas More written from the Tower of London in 1534 and 1535, letters of German Lutheran theologian Dietrich Bonhoffer written from a Nazi prison from 1939 through 1945, and Dr. Martin Luther King Jr.'s "Letter from Birmingham City Jail," written on April 16, 1963.[3] Both More and Bonhoffer were eventually executed, and King was assassinated, making their prison writings all the more poignant.

Religious prison writings have been composed by a wide variety of men and women, including Catholics, Puritans, Quakers, Baptists, and others. W. Clark Gilpin, University of Chicago Divinity School professor, noted, "Such letters are—at one level—extraordinary dramatic documents of personal history, which may be addressed to government officials in protest; to religious communities in encouragement; to other prisoners in solidarity; or to parents, spouses, and children in consolation."[4] Gilpin argued that these prison writings are more than personal correspondence but "acts of testimony, a bearing of witness by persons who believe themselves to be unjustly incarcerated for their fidelity to conscience and religious principle."[5]

JOSEPH SMITH IN PRISON

Like the first-century New Testament Church, the restored Church of Jesus Christ has experienced its own persecution over the course of its history and especially in its early years. In some cases, members and leaders have been arrested, confined to prison, and murdered. The Prophet Joseph Smith was among the earliest

Saints subjected to persecution and prosecution. He was familiar with arresting officers, lawyers, judges, and prisons. In recent years, scholars have become aware of more than two hundred legal cases in which Joseph Smith was involved. Indeed, it is scarcely an exaggeration to say that Joseph lived his active life—and eventually gave his life—in the shadow of the law. During his incarceration in Liberty Jail between 1838 and 1839, he wrote a number of letters. Extracts from a rather long letter dated March 20, 1839, were eventually included in the Doctrine and Covenants as sections 121–23. Like some of Paul's prison letters, these extracts have been canonized, becoming part of sacred scripture for all generations, and are notable for their power and depth.

Joseph Smith in Liberty Jail, used by permission of Greg Olsen, Art Publishing, Inc.

Another series of letters, written during a period of exile in September 1842, were also added to the canon (see D&C 127–28). At the end of his life, while in Carthage Jail, just before he was martyred by an armed mob, Joseph Smith wrote other letters that have been preserved.[6] Prison writings did not cease among the members of the Church with the martyrdom of Joseph Smith. This genre of Christian literature witnessed a phenomenal period of creativity and growth when the U.S. government prosecuted thousands of Latter-day Saints for their practice of plural marriage in the second half of the 1880s.[7]

FEDERAL LEGAL WAR AGAINST THE CHURCH

Barely understood and often demonized during the second half of the nineteenth century, the Latter-day Saints were characterized as an alien group within the boundaries of the United States. Because of their polygamist traditions, they were compared with Africans and Asians, peoples that white Protestant Anglo-Americans felt were unable, unfit, and unworthy to govern themselves.[8] Few people or institutions challenged these blatantly prejudicial depictions. Mainline newspapers, churches, reform groups, and political parties not only encouraged but also invented and perpetuated such comparisons.[9]

In the waning years of the federal reconstruction of the South, the eyes of Washington DC's politicians increasingly turned westward to Utah. In this setting, the federal government began its concentrated legal attack on the Church. The Saints, however, launched a spirited counterattack of their own. University of Pennsylvania law professor Sarah Barringer Gordon argued, "Resistance to the laws of man galvanized the Saints in Utah. The virulence of attacks from outside (and, especially after the completion of the transcontinental railroad in 1869, from non-Mormons within) Utah were met and matched by the Mormons. . . . [Reformers] did not anticipate the power and religious conviction of Mormon resistance, or the ability of Mormon leaders to articulate positive cultural and legal arguments in favor of polygamy."[10] She added, "The Mormons' strategy was offensive as well as defensive, socially and politically astute, and legally sophisticated."[11]

Nevertheless, argued Thomas G. Alexander, professor emeritus, Brigham Young University, a coalition of "Evangelical Protestants, women's groups, and other moralists . . . anxious to thwart a sinful practice destructive to the American family . . . made polygamy into a front-running moral issue. . . . [U.S.] President Hayes, a strict Protestant moralist, asked Congress [in 1880] to take all political power—voting, jury service, and officeholding—from those 'who practice and uphold the crime' of polygamy."[12] While sometimes dismissed as nothing more than a rallying cry by non-Mormons in Utah to generate sympathy in the East, "polygamy was actually central to the federal government's legal campaign against the Mormons and formed an important part of the ideology of the GOP politicians who dominated post-Civil War politics."[13]

Gordon highlighted the results of the federal legal conflict with the Saints: "There are approximately 2,500 criminal cases in the [Utah Territory] court records from 1871 to 1896. . . . More than 95 percent are for sexual crimes [polygamy, cohabitation, and fornication]. . . . It is, literally, unique in American legal history."[14] BYU history professor Kathryn M. Daynes added, "Between 1884 and 1895, over a thousand men were convicted of a crime relating

"Within the Gates," Utah Penitentiary, May 30, 1887, photograph by Charles R. Savage, used by permission, Church History Library, Salt Lake City, Utah. A group of prisoners pose between bunkhouses 1 and 2 (*left*) and the dining hall (*right*).

to plural marriage."[15] Many, but not all, were incarcerated in the 1880s and early 1890s.

During imprisonment, many Latter-day Saints wrote in diaries and autograph books and corresponded with family, friends, Church leaders, and others. As a result, a rather significant body of prison writings has survived the intervening years and is held in private possession and in various institutional archives and libraries. These important records contain reflections about the challenges of life, faith, commitment, and prison experiences of men and women who chose to obey their conscience rather than laws believed to be unjust.

Initially, female authors and lecturers who emphasized the depravity and barbaric nature of polygamy brought the Mormon practice to the public's attention in the 1850s. However, these critics "were increasingly marginalized, as male legislators, lawyers, and judges emerged as key players" in the battle against plural marriage in the decades that followed.[16] Alexander suggested that this was primarily because only men voted, passed legislation, or held offices as marshals, judges, prosecuting attorneys, and prison wardens.[17] Still, books by former Latter-day Saint women, such as Ann Eliza Young and Fanny Stenhouse, continued to sell well, and their lectures drew large crowds that included prominent government officials.[18] Even Ulysses S. Grant, the president of the United States, attended one of these lectures.[19]

Because federal lawmakers saw plural marriage as a moral deviation that threatened not only the traditional, monogamous family unit but also the progress of Western civilization, whose survival hinged on the success of the nuclear family, they decided to use state coercion to enforce their particular values.[20] Federal action centered on the abolition of plural marriage in an effort to free women from perceived bondage and domination by male Church leaders. However, when it became apparent that Latter-day Saint women, now identified as "willing victims," supported plural marriage, the government became less interested in them and passed legislation to disenfranchise Latter-day Saint voters, bar them from

Lorenzo Snow provided encouragement and reflections in a number of autograph albums while in prison. This poem to Maria Burrows on November 2, 1886, shows his distinctive signature written in indelible purple pencil, which he preferred because it was virtually impossible to erase. This poem was also included in Lorenzo Snow's record book. See pages 70–71 herein. Used by permission, Church History Library.

holding public office and serving on juries, strip their children of inheritance rights, and disincorporate the Church itself.[21]

Congress's first attempt to eradicate plural marriage was the Morrill Act of 1862. Never before, one legal historian argued, had the federal government "assumed such supervisory power over structures of private authority."[22] The Morrill Act included provisions that made plural marriage (termed "bigamy") punishable by a five-hundred-dollar fine and imprisonment up to five years. The act also annulled the Utah Territorial Legislature's act of incorporating The Church of Jesus Christ of Latter-day Saints and stipulated that no church or charitable organization in any territory could "acquire or hold real estate" in excess of $50,000.[23]

However, the act's antipolygamy provisions proved very difficult to implement. First, it appears that President Abraham Lincoln, who was prosecuting a war, was unenthusiastic about enforcing the legislation. Additionally, Latter-day Saints controlled jury selection in Utah, making it nearly impossible to find someone who would convict a fellow member of the Church. Also, territorial law granted original jurisdiction in criminal and civil cases to the probate courts, which were in the control of Latter-day Saints.[24]

In 1874, the U.S. Congress attempted to overcome Mormon resistance with the Poland Act. Law professors Edwin B. Firmage and Richard C. Mangrum observed that the act "resolved the rivalry between territorial and federal judicial officers"[25] by restricting probate court jurisdiction, divesting the territorial attorney and marshal of much of their authority, and changing the jury selection process.[26]

This shift in control was clearly demonstrated in the 1874–79 trials of George Reynolds, secretary to the First Presidency.[27] In a carefully planned legal maneuver, the Church chose Reynolds, a young, less-prominent member of the Church who was married to only two women, to test the constitutionality of the 1862 antibigamy legislation. The Church relied on the 1857 *Dred Scott* decision because it "continued to be good law to the extent that it limited the power of the federal government to regulate 'domestic' issues in the territories."[28] Nathan Oman, a law professor at William and Mary, observed, "The Mormons argued in effect that these limitations protected local autonomy in matters of faith."[29]

Nevertheless, "the Supreme Court reframed the issue to ask whether Mormons' religious belief in polygamy meant that the law in question violated their free exercise of religion under the First Amendment."[30] Eventually, the high court ruled that although Congress could not legislate against religious beliefs and opinions, it could make laws against certain religious practices. It therefore sustained the essence of a Utah District Court's ruling that sentenced Reynolds to prison for violating the law against plural marriage.[31] This was a major blow to LDS legal efforts "because it cleared the constitutional road for convictions . . . [and] provided the political impetus to pass laws facilitating them."[32]

In a rare political and historical circumstance resulting from the assassination of James A. Garfield in 1881, three U.S. presidents (Hays, Garfield, and Arthur) demanded that the U.S. Congress act on the Mormon problem—all within one year. Under Republican leadership, Congress did act with Vermont senator George F. Edmunds's comprehensive antipolygamy bill. During the bitter debate, some senators voiced strong reservations about some of the bill's provisions. For example, Senator J. T. Morgan "stated that he was 'not willing to persecute a Mormon at the expense of the Constitution of the United States.'"[33] Edward Leo Lyman, professor emeritus of history at Victor Valley College, noted, "On the other side of the question, Edmunds allegedly argued that 'there is no constitution but the will of the people.'"[34] Eventually the Edmunds Act became law in 1882. Although the 1862 Morrill Act outlawed plural marriage, the Edmunds Act was the first piece of legislation to give federal officials the means effectively to arrest and prosecute those engaged in plural marriage. The Morrill Act had required prosecutors to demonstrate that a man had married more than one woman. This proved to be difficult, if not impossible, because marriage records were not kept in Utah at the time and the relatively few witnesses to such marriages—generally performed in the Endowment House or Utah temples—often "preferred to face contempt charges rather than reveal information related to temple ordinances."[35]

The Edmunds Act sidestepped the issue by requiring prosecutors to demonstrate only that a man "cohabited" with more than one wife, that is, "held them [two or more women] out to the world, by his language or conduct, or both, as his wives."[36] No longer did the government need a record or witness of the marriage to convict a man practicing plural marriage. For federal officials bent on eradicating plural marriage, virtually any contact between an alleged polygamist and his wives could be considered conduct reflective of cohabitation and used as evidence in court. This allowed the government to convict many Latter-day Saints on the less severe charge of "unlawful cohabitation" instead of polygamy.[37] In fact, only twelve men were convicted of polygamy per se between 1884 and 1895.[38]

Historical records suggest that Latter-day Saints respected federal officials who performed their duties and responsibilities with fairness, but many federal judges and officers sent to Utah during this period were openly hostile appointees bent on the reconstruction of Utah's unique society.[39] For example, President Chester A. Arthur appointed Charles S. Zane as chief justice of the Supreme Court of Utah Territory because, as his advisers knew, "Zane would interpret the Edmunds Act in the desired manner."[40] Later, in Utah, Zane told a Mormon defendant, "If you do not submit, of course, you must take the consequences, but the will of the American people and the law will go on and grind your institution to powder."[41] Lyman observed, "The territorial judges embarked on the 'grinding' process by adopting a set of judicial tactics that included selecting grand jury members according to their stated biases against Mormonism, seating all-Gentile trial

"Governor Murray and U.S. Officials 1884," used by permission, Utah State Historical Society, Salt Lake City, Utah. These federally appointed Utah Territory officials led the government's efforts to arrest, prosecute, and imprison Latter-day Saints who practiced plural marriage. *Left to right:* Orlando W. Powers, associate justice; Elwin A. Ireland, U.S. marshal; Eli H. Murray, governor; Charles S. Zane, chief justice; William H. Dickson, U.S. attorney; and Jacob S. Boreman, associate justice.

juries, imprisoning witnesses—including women—who refused to testify, denying bonds, and levying lengthy prison sentences on those convicted."[42]

A challenging aspect of the court system in Utah was the relationship between the district courts and the Utah Territorial Supreme Court. Utah had been divided into three districts with federally appointed judges presiding in each. However, these same three judges served together as justices of the Utah Territorial Supreme Court, which reviewed "their own lower court decisions on appeal."[43] Consequently, Latter-day Saints believed they could not receive a fair trial and review on appeal in Utah courts, where the same federally appointed officials sat in both courts.

At first, the federal government primarily targeted members of the First Presidency and the Quorum of the Twelve Apostles, believing that arresting, convicting, and incarcerating prominent leaders would force them to abandon plural marriage.[44] However, Church leaders decided to avoid certain arrest and imprisonment by starting life on the "Mormon Underground"—an allusion to the "Underground Railroad," a vast but informal network of safe houses and secret routes that led escaped black slaves to freedom in the North and Canada.[45] This strategy included seeking refuge in various secret hideouts, both at home and in settlements beyond Salt Lake City and in mission fields beyond Utah.[46] This effort began what has been described as "the longest continuously sustained record of planned civil disobedience in the history of [the United States]."[47]

The Church's successful efforts to thwart federal officials forced the government to adjust its tactics. Instead of hoping to imprison well-known Church leaders, the government apparently decided to arrest, convict, and incarcerate every man they could who was practicing plural marriage and therefore expanded its operation to include rural Mormon villages and communities beyond Utah's boundaries.[48] This hunt for "cohabs" (men suspected of cohabitation) sent hundreds of Latter-day Saints, including men, women, and children, into hiding.[49] Eventually, some Latter-day Saints moved to Mexico and western Canada in order to avoid arrest. Mormon historians Leonard J. Arrington and Davis Bitton noted, "Life on the underground was a wearying cycle of travel, hardship, and close escapes."[50] Nevertheless, the decision to avoid capture raised the cost for each and every conviction, significantly forcing the federal government to pay dearly in its efforts to enforce the law. Ironically, this played into the hands of the local U.S. marshals, who knew that "increased arrests would enhance their salaries and expense account."[51]

In 1884, Rudger Clawson became the first Latter-day Saint "convicted and imprisoned for violation of the Edmunds law."[52]

He was sentenced to six months' imprisonment for unlawful cohabitation (often identified as "u.c." in diaries and letters) and three and a half years for polygamy for a combined sentence of four years.[53] In the following year another thirty-eight men were convicted for cohabitation. In 1886 the number rose to 107 men convicted for cohabitation, including the first prominent Church leader, Lorenzo Snow (1814–1901), a senior member of the Quorum of the Twelve Apostles.[54]

Prisoners in the Utah Penitentiary, August 1885, photograph by John P. Soul, used by permission, Church History Library. *Left to right:* Francis A. Brown, Freddy Self, Moroni Brown, Amos Milton Musser, George H. Kellogg, Parley P. Pratt Jr., Rudger Clawson, Job Pingree. Self and Kellogg were not incarcerated for plural marriage. Rudger Clawson acted as Lorenzo Snow's scribe in prison.

LORENZO SNOW'S LIFE

Lorenzo Snow joined the Church on June 23, 1836, in Kirtland, Ohio.[55] Like many other male converts, he served several short missions to various counties in Ohio, Illinois, and Kentucky from 1837 to 1839. In 1840, he traveled to the British Isles to begin an extended missionary effort through 1843. After returning to the United States, the thirty-year-old bachelor married two cousins on the same day in October 1844, becoming the first Latter-day Saint

Lorenzo Snow, about 1886, from a glass-plate negative by Charles W. Carter, used by permission, Church History Library.

to leap directly from bachelorhood into plural marriage. He married several other times in Illinois and was sealed to four of his wives in the Nauvoo Temple on the same day, January 19, 1846.[56]

Lorenzo Snow made his way to the Salt Lake Valley in 1848, a year after Brigham Young designated it as the gathering place.

In the following year, he was called to the Quorum of the Twelve Apostles, an assignment Lorenzo Snow held until 1898, when he became the fifth President of the Church. Between 1849 and 1852, he joined other Church leaders in opening new missions in continental Europe. He personally inaugurated the Italian Mission in the Piedmont region among the Waldensians (or Waldenses or Vaudois), a Protestant group living in the foothills and valleys of the French-Italian Alps.

In 1853, after his return to Utah, Snow was called to preside in Box Elder County in northern Utah. He moved his growing family to Brigham City by the summer of 1855. Later he served a short mission to the Hawaiian Islands beginning in 1864 and made an extended visit to Europe and the Holy Land beginning in 1872.

By 1882, when the Edmunds Act became law in the United States, Lorenzo Snow had married ten times.[57] His wives included Harriet Amelia and Charlotte Squires (married in October 1844 or January 1845), Eleanor Houtz (married on January 1, 1845), Mary Adaline and Hannah Goddard (married on January 19, 1845), Sarah Ann Prichard (married on April 21, 1845), Caroline Horton (married on October 9, 1853), Phoebe Amelia Woodruff (married on April 4, 1859), Mary Elizabeth Houtz (unknown date, but likely before spring 1859), and Sarah Minnie Ephramina Jensen (married on June 12, 1871).[58]

Two wives had died by the time the Edmunds Act became law—Charlotte Squires in 1850 and Caroline Horton in 1857. Additionally, Hannah Goddard had deserted Lorenzo Snow shortly after their marriage in 1845.[59] In addition to seven living wives, the Snow family consisted of many children, ranging from age two to age thirty-five (not including Mary Goddard's three children from an earlier marriage), and numerous grandchildren.[60]

Although the details of these marriages were most likely unknown to many, it was well known that Snow practiced plural marriage, having established four separate homes in Brigham City for his family. The main home, known as the "Big House," was

The family of Lorenzo and Minnie Snow, about 1888, used by permission, Church History Library. *Left to right:* Minnie Jensen Snow, LeRoi Clarence Snow, Minnie Mabelle Snow, and Lorenzo Lamont Snow.

located at 250 North Main Street in Brigham City with separate apartments for three wives. Minnie had moved into the fourth home, a new brick house on the corner of First West and Forest on the back side of the block of the Big House in 1880.[61]

In the wake of the 1882 Edmunds Law, Lorenzo Snow and his wives decided by "mutual consent" to live "in accordance with the requirements of that law, and this, too, without violating any principle or object embraced in the law of celestial marriage."[62] This meant ending physical intimacy with all his wives except Minnie, the wife with the youngest children (LeRoi Clarence was five and Minnie Mabelle was two) and the only one still bearing children. Lorenzo and Minnie had three additional children after 1882: Cora Jeane on February 16, 1883, Lorenzo Lamont on August 26, 1885, and Rhea Lucile on November 5, 1896.

LORENZO SNOW AND THE ANTIPOLYGAMY CRUSADE

As mentioned, the passage of the Edmunds Act made it easier to obtain convictions on the charge of unlawful cohabitation. Additionally, the interpretation that any type of contact with more than one wife constituted a violation of the law meant that Snow's ongoing efforts to provide for all his wives—even though he was living with only one of them—could be considered grounds for prosecution. In May 1885, Snow was warned that he might be arrested.[63] As a result, he decided to leave Brigham City for a season. Like other Latter-day Saints on the Underground, Snow used code words in his communications to hide his identity and location. For example, in July 1885 he sent a letter to "Angus," written from "Jerusalem," and signed "Ecclesiastes."[64] Snow was in San Francisco in July 1885 when the First Presidency called him to serve a short mission among the native peoples in the Northwest, including Idaho and Wyoming.[65]

Lorenzo Snow returned to Brigham City on September 24, 1885.[66] That same month Charles Zane, chief justice of the Utah Territorial Supreme Court and also a district court justice, began instructing grand juries that they could indict prisoners on smaller "segregated" periods—in other words, a man could be indicted for each year, month, or week of cohabitation. This aggressive interpretation meant a man could be imprisoned for life, transforming "unlawful cohabitation, which was technically a minor misdemeanor, into a major criminal offence."[67]

J. W. Greenman, John Cudihee, E A.Ireland, E A. Franks, L.B.S.Miller, T.Smith, J.Gleason, O Vandercook, Chief Deputy. U S.D.Marshal. U.S.Marshal. U. S D. M. Chief Clerk. U.S.D.M. U.S D.M. U.S.Deputy Marshal.

U.S. marshal E. A. Ireland, marshal office chief clerk L. B. S. Miller (*center*), and the six U.S. deputy marshals that arrested Lorenzo Snow on November 20, 1885. Illustration from M. Koch's *His Ten Wives* (1887).

On November 19, 1885, a complaint was issued against Snow before U.S. commissioner T. J. Black, a judicial officer responsible for a variety of duties, including issuing summons and warrants. The complaint charged Snow with cohabiting with seven women in 1883, 1884, and the first eleven months of 1885: "Adaline [Goddard] Snow, Sarah [Prichard] Snow, Harriet [Squires] Snow, Eleanor [Houtz] Snow, Mary H[outz] Snow, Phoebe W[oodruff] Snow, and Minnie Jensen Snow."[68] A warrant for his arrest was issued to deputy federal marshal Oscar Vandercook. Sometime after midnight on November 20, 1885, six federal officers, including Vandercook, "silently left Ogden in several conveyances and drove to Brigham City" and in a predawn raid found Snow hiding in a secret compartment in his home.[69] LeRoi Snow noted that a "group of young men came forward and threatened to prevent the deputies from taking Apostle Snow (part of a group of forty men who had promised to protect him with their lives)."[70] However, Snow did not want them to interfere, so the arrest and departure from Brigham City proceeded without incident.

Shortly thereafter, in December 1885, the *Deseret News* reported, "In the First district Court, at Ogden, yesterday, before Judge Powers, Apostle Lorenzo Snow, was arraigned on three indictments, charging him with unlawful cohabitation with his wives . . . The defendant was not represented by attorney, and was allowed until Monday to enter his plea."[71]

Snow's first trial in the First District Court in Ogden began in December 1885. Everyone,

PROSECUTING ATTORNEY VICTOR BEIRBOWER.

Victor "Vic" Beirbower, prosecuting attorney in the Lorenzo Snow trial. Illustration from M. Koch's *His Ten Wives* (1887).

including federal officials, knew that this "case was of more than ordinary importance because it was a more than ordinary person who was on trial—one of the most eminent persons of the Church."[72] B. Carmon Hardy, professor emeritus of history at California State University–Fullerton, noted, "When Apostle Lorenzo Snow was apprehended and placed on trial, the prosecuting attorney, Victor Beirbower, predicted that if Snow and others were found guilty and sent to prison, Church leaders would find it convenient to have a revelation setting aside the commandment on polygamy. Numbers of revelations were forthcoming—more, perhaps, than at any time since the death of Joseph Smith. But the messages invariably encouraged perseverance, spoke of the imminence of final things, and urged continued allegiance to the principle."[73]

The trial was widely publicized and attended by some of the largest crowds the court in Ogden had ever seen. A short book, *His*

Ten Wives: The Travels, Trial and Conviction of the Mormon Apostle, Lorenzo Snow, was published in 1887, recounting the events from a prejudicial view. The key players in the drama included assistant U.S. district attorney Victor Beirbower, recently selected by district attorney William H. Dickson to fill the position; Snow's primary attorney, Franklin S. Richards (general council for the Church); and district judge Orlando W. Powers, who also served as an associate judge on the Territorial Supreme Court.

From the beginning, Lorenzo Snow believed he had complied with the Edmunds law by living with only one wife in a separate home. However, Beirbower argued that any support of a plural wife constituted cohabitation. Daynes summarized the situation: "Apostle Snow found that his living solely with his youngest wife, Minnie, did not prevent his conviction. One witness testified at his trial that he had seen Snow visiting the house of his wife Sarah, sitting with her at the theater, and riding with her in a carriage. These acts, along with his financial support of Sarah and their reputation in the community as husband and wife, were sufficient to find the apostle guilty of unlawfully cohabiting with Minnie."[74]

The non-Mormon jury convicted Snow of the first charge of cohabitation on December 31, 1885.[75] The *New York Times* reported the news on its front page: "Apostle Snow Convicted."[76] After the conviction, Snow's attorney argued that it "barred further prosecutions, but the trial court brushed that argument aside and proceeded with the selection of a second jury."[77] This jury convicted Snow on January 5, 1886, on two additional counts of "unlawful cohabitation."[78] Again the *New York Times* announced the decision.[79]

Shortly before sentencing, Snow spoke to the Saints in Brigham City: "I go to prison with the full assurance that I can serve God and His purposes—magnify my calling and prove to the world, my faith and sincerity in the principles I have taught, during fifty years, among many nations—that Jesus is the Son of God—that He has revealed His Priesthood, and the fulness of the ancient Gospel, and established His Church by revelation."[80] He concluded his discourse: "In a few days I must leave family, kind friends and associates with whom I have spent so many pleasant hours in 'The City I love so well'—proceed to Ogden—receive my sentence, then retire to private life, within my prison walls, for 'The word of God and testimony of Jesus.'"[81]

On January 16, 1886, Powers sentenced Lorenzo Snow to the maximum penalty allowed under the law—three consecutive six-month terms (one for each charge of cohabitation) and three fines of three hundred dollars (also one for each), totaling nine hundred dollars. Charles Lowell Walker, a member of the Church living in southern Utah, recorded in his diary, "Apostle Lorenzo Snow received his sentence from Judge Powers, 18 months in the Penitentiary and 9 hundred dollars fine. Lorenzo Snow made an able and eloquent speech before the court and bore his testimony to the divinity of the work of God and Holy institutions and ordinances of the gospel, which will stand against Judge Powers and the United States officials before the Bar of the Great God at the Last Day."[82] At the time, Lorenzo Snow was the highest-ranking Church official to be arrested and convicted under the Edmunds Act. His conviction represented a significant victory for federal officials in their efforts against plural marriage.

Snow appealed his convictions to the Utah Territorial Supreme Court, arguing that his breach of the law had been a "single continuous offense" over three years rather than "a series of [three] discrete offenses" and that he should therefore be prosecuted and convicted for at most only one count of cohabitation.[83]

Between the trial and the court hearing on this appeal, the Young Ladies' Mutual Improvement Association in Brigham City honored Lorenzo Snow. In their tribute they said, "Should God, our Heavenly Father, see proper in his allwise providence to suffer our enemies to drag you to prison, it will be for righteousness sake, and He will glorify you in glorifying himself, through the testimony of your sacrifice. We pray Him to bless you with all that will be most conducive to your comfort, and we will continually pray that God will give you strength according to your day."[84]

Not surprisingly, the Utah Territorial Supreme Court, consisting of Charles S. Zane, Jacob S. Boreman, and Orlando W. Powers (the judge who originally sentenced him), rejected Lorenzo Snow's argument on February 6, 1886.[85] The court noted, "The evidence against the defendant shows one of the most aggravated cases and worst examples of polygamy."[86] Boreman stated, "In the case under consideration, we find a state of affairs which, by the facts developed in this class of trials, is coming to be well known to have a common existence in this territory."[87] Powers added his comments, "The American idea of government is founded on the Christian idea of home,—where one father and one mother, each equal of the other, happy in the consequences of mutual and eternal affections, rear about the hearthstone an intelligent and God-fearing family."[88]

Franklin S. Richards, May 29, 1888, photograph by Charles Parker, Washington DC, used by permission, Utah State Historical Society. Richards acted as the Church's general counsel and was Snow's personal attorney.

Lorenzo Snow's primary attorney, Franklin S. Richards, and a second attorney, George Ticknor Curtis, a prominent non-LDS Washington lawyer, appealed the case to the U.S. Supreme Court. Lorenzo Snow wrote Richards, saying, "In learning of your success in securing appeal in my three cases to the U.S. Supreme Court, and promise of bails, my pleasure was only equaled by my surprise and astonishment. While reading your communication, in the presence of some of my family, and several callers, the close of each paragraph, was greeted with clapping of hands, and other demonstrations of delight. I hope that the final outcome will prove a source of relief, and rejoicing to hundreds, as well as myself, who are interested in the questions involved in the issue. . . . I remain, Your Brother in the New and Everlasting Covenant. Lorenzo Snow."[89]

In the meantime, Snow decided to begin his sentence in the Utah Territorial Penitentiary, under federal control since 1871. On the evening of March 12, 1886, Snow rode to the penitentiary in Sugar House, an area southeast of Salt Lake City (the current site of Sugar House Park). The prison admission record noted that Lorenzo Snow was 5 feet 9 inches tall, weighed 155 pounds, had a dark complexion, light grey eyes, and was a "preacher" by occupation.[90]

Abraham H. Cannon explained Snow's motivation to begin his incarceration in a diary entry dated March 12, 1886: "Apostle Lorenzo Snow today voluntarily delivered himself up to the U.S. marshal for confinement in the 'Pen,' so that his case, now pending before the U.S. Supreme Court, might be advanced on the calendar. His case is to test the validity of the segregating process now in vogue."[91]

Territorial Penitentiary, Sugar House, Looking East, 1886, oil on canvas, 11″ × 22″, painting by Francis Treseder. Gift from Nancy Roney and Kalleen Lund, Orem, Utah, used by permission, Springville Museum of Art.

LORENZO SNOW'S PRISON EXPERIENCE

Under prison rules, inmates' hair was cut once a month and facial hair shaved once a week, but Lorenzo Snow received permission to retain his beard after two doctors, John D. Cornham and J. P. Allen, wrote to the warden advising that shaving his beard and cutting his hair would adversely affect his health.[92] This concession was not insignificant, as the second half of the nineteenth century witnessed the dramatic increase in facial hair in Western Europe and the United States. The period is sometimes called the "Golden Age of Beards," a time when a beard was a primary sign of masculinity, wisdom, and patriarchal authority and honor. Having one's beard shaved was considered a degrading personal affront. Many Mormon prisoners were not as fortunate as Lorenzo Snow. All in all, Snow said he was treated with "marked consideration and respect."[93]

Like other prisoners, Snow experienced cold in the winter, extreme heat and bedbugs in the summer, and a Spartan diet of bread, coffee, tea, boiled potatoes, soup, nondescript meat, and hash.[94] The rhythms of prison life rarely changed—monotony was the prisoners' worst enemy. Those prisoners who helped cook were up by 5:15 a.m., and the remaining prisoners were awakened just before 7:00. The warden, however, was often lenient with the "brethren," and they did not have to get up until 7:30. Prisoners had access to the bathhouse, where two tubs could be found—bathers brought their own water or paid someone to do the job. They were required to take a bath once a week in the summers and once every two weeks during the winter. Breakfast was served at 8:00 in the dining hall, a forty-five by twenty-foot plank structure with bathroom and washroom attached. The basic meal seems to have always included bread, while gifts from the outside such as butter, honey, and preserves occasionally made the experience more enjoyable. Lunch was served at 12:15 p.m., and supper was served at 4:45 p.m. The prisoners were sent back to the bunkhouse at 5:15 p.m. Snow's fellow prisoner John Nicholson noted, "As soon

"Looking into the Utah Penitentiary from the Wall," May 30, 1887, photograph by Charles R. Savage, used by permission, Church History Library. The dining hall (*foreground*), the building containing bunkhouses 1 and 2 (*left*) and bunkhouse 3 (*upper right*).

as the prisoners are within, the heavy iron door is closed and the ponderous bars are adjusted."[95] Talking ceased at 9:00 p.m. The guards passed by every fifteen minutes throughout the night to check on the prisoners.

Every prisoner was required to take his daily turn sweeping his bunkhouse and weekly turn scrubbing the floor. Additionally, they were assigned to "police" the prison yard—a little less then one acre inside the prison walls (twenty feet high and four feet wide). Finally, the prisoners were assigned turns to clean the dining room and serve as waiters.

Some prisoners brought their own mattresses; others brought books, writing instruments, and paper. One item often mentioned is the lack of contemporary news, as newspapers were prohibited (though some diaries mention newspapers on occasion). Abraham Cannon said he did not realize what a "great blessing having the news" was until he was denied access to it in prison.[96]

Rudger Clawson, the first and only Mormon prisoner incarcerated for plural marriage in 1884, must have felt alone in the facility, a wholly foreign world to most Latter-day Saints who had never been arrested or incarcerated before. Coarse and profane language, fighting, and thieving were the rule instead of the exception. As prosecution for cohabitation continued, the number of imprisoned Latter-day Saints increased dramatically. Abraham Cannon, who began his own sentence only a few days after Lorenzo Snow, reported that of the 150 prisoners in the Utah penitentiary, 50 were Church members.[97] By June 1887 there were nearly one hundred Latter-day Saints in the "Pen," making Mormons the majority of the prison population.

Cannon observed that as a result of the increasing numbers of Mormon prisoners, it "is not nearly as unpleasant as it might be or as I expected it would be."[98] Nevertheless, there was some friction between the two distinct groups: the "toughs" and the "cohabs." However, diarists reflect from time to time on the kindness many non-LDS prisoners showed the older Mormon prisoners. The increasing number of Latter-day Saints also seems to have changed the culture

Territorial Penitentiary, Sugar House, Looking West, 1886, oil on canvas, 11″ × 22″, painting by Francis Treseder. Gift from Nancy Roney and Kalleen Lund, Orem, Utah, used by permission, Springville Museum of Art. This painting highlights the dining hall (*left*), the building that contained bunkhouses 1 and 2 (*center*) and the separate bunkhouse 3 (*right*).

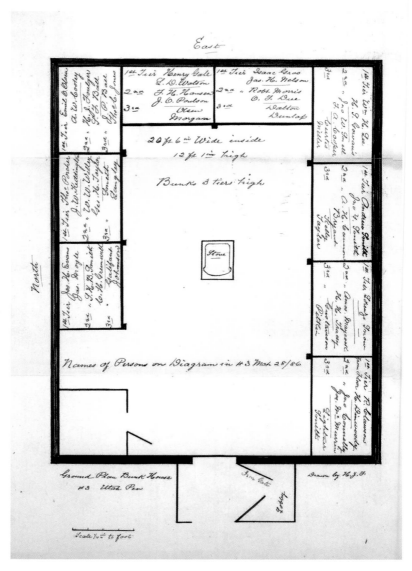

"Ground Plan Bunk House #3 Utah Pen," by Herbert J. Foulger, March 28, 1886, used by permission, L. Tom Perry Special Collections, Harold B. Lee Library, Brigham Young University, Provo, UT. Foulger, incarcerated from February 26 through September 2, 1886, prepared this drawing of bunkhouse number 3, showing bed assignments. Lorenzo Snow's is noted third from the top on the right. The lobby is located at the bottom of the drawing (note the iron gate that was closed each night to secure the prisoners).

within the prison system in many significant and discernable ways, which was generally noticed and appreciated by prison officials. For example, Clawson recalled, "The guards felt as much at ease among the prisoners as they possibly could have done at home. The marshal abandoned the practice of driving the men into one corner of the yard like so many cattle when visiting the prison."[99]

Two large wood buildings stood near the dining hall. The first building was divided into bunkhouses 1 and 2. The second building was called bunkhouse number 3 and had been built in the summer of 1885. This latest addition to the prison measured nearly twenty-one by twenty-seven feet and housed about fifty-two inmates, including Lorenzo Snow, Rudger Clawson, Abraham Cannon, and other members of the Church. The prisoners slept in a three-tier bunk bed (six feet six inches long and four feet six inches wide) with two people assigned to a bed. Early on, Snow did not have a bunk mate, a privilege that must have made his stay more comfortable. Unfortunately, he was unable to retain this privilege during his entire sentence as the number of inmates increased over time.

On December 4, 1886, Lorenzo Snow wrote a poem, "My Boudoir," describing his bedroom (see pages [77]–[78]). This was published just before his release in the February 1887 *Juvenile Instructor* and simply signed "Cohab."[100] The published poem is slightly different from the version in the record book.

'Tis, no doubt, you well remember
My neat, cosy sleeping chamber,
Yet our friends 'twill not displease
Somewhat to know—their hearts 'twill ease,

So thus their fears entire disarm—
How nice we're fixed by "Uncle Sam."
Though oft he fails to full comply
With all we wish, all wants supply;

Yet him we hold in high disdain,
The poor ingrate that would complain
Two feet, if add two inches more,
My Boudoir starts from building floor;

Just four feet wide, its length 'tis seven,
Though much preferred if eight by 'leven.
For floor, rough boards on scantling stayed,
Wire cot o'er this correctly laid; . . .

Thick, heavy cloth our heads behind
Divide two beds, to four assigned;
Below, at foot, board wide and strong
Preserves our rights, none venture wrong.

Arguments in Lorenzo Snow's appeal to the U.S. Supreme Court were delivered on April 28, 1886, shortly after his incarceration began. However, the court decided in May 1886 that it did not have jurisdiction. In general, the United States Supreme Court was empowered to hear certain types of cases. The justices decided Snow's appeal was not among them. Abraham Cannon noted, "Bro. Snow seemed to take the decision quite calmly though it must be a severe blow to a man of his age to think of remaining here still a solid 13 months."[101]

Snow maintained his health while incarcerated, with the exception of a head cold at the beginning of his sentence.[102] He noted on June 13, 1886, "My health all along has been universally good, better I believe, than at any time during the past two years. . . . Every day I make it a practice to take exercise by walking around the yard, from a mile to a mile and half nine times round the yard makes one mile. I am considered one of the finest and fastest of walkers, and am constantly tendered compliments on my remarkably healthy appearance, and buoyant spirits; in fact I am a surprise to myself. I [feel] that I owe much of this to the faith and prayers of the Saints, and feel very grateful to them and the Lord."[103] During his walk, others

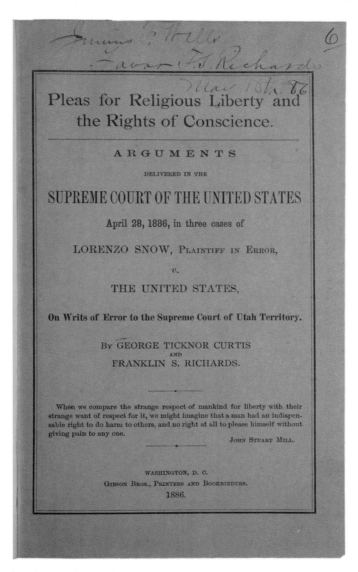

Pleas for Religious Liberty and the Rights of Conscience.

ARGUMENTS

DELIVERED IN THE

SUPREME COURT OF THE UNITED STATES

April 28, 1886, in three cases of

LORENZO SNOW, Plaintiff in Error,

v.

THE UNITED STATES,

On Writs of Error to the Supreme Court of Utah Territory.

By GEORGE TICKNOR CURTIS
AND
FRANKLIN S. RICHARDS.

When we compare the strange respect of mankind for liberty with their
strange want of respect for it, we might imagine that a man had an indispen-
sable right to do harm to others, and no right at all to please himself without
giving pain to any one.
JOHN STUART MILL.

WASHINGTON, D. C.
GIBSON BROS., PRINTERS AND BOOKBINDERS.
1886.

Pleas for Religious Liberty and the Rights of Conscience (1886), used by permission, L. Tom
Perry Special Collections. George Ticknor Curtis, a Harvard Law School graduate and
defender of Latter-day Saint rights, worked with Franklin S. Richards, general counsel
for the Church in Lorenzo Snow's first appeal to the U.S. Supreme Court. They prepared
the written arguments in the case. Later, they were successful in overturning the Utah
court's definition of separate incidents of violation of the 1882 Edmunds Law, in Snow's
second appeal to the court.

often accompanied Snow. One inmate noted in his diary with pride, "I had the privilege to walk arm in arm with Lorenzo Snow."[104]

While clearly wishing he were elsewhere, Lorenzo Snow nevertheless made good use of his time in prison. He organized classes among the inmates in reading, writing, math, and bookkeeping. One prisoner reported, "Some six weeks ago Apostle Snow feeling a deepening interest in the school, kindly volunteered to give two lectures a week on grammar. A class of fifteen members was organized and has since been under his kind and able tutelage and it has brought new life into the study and his lectures are looked forward to with the warmest interest. His able, kind, and genial manners have found way into the hearts of the entire school."[105]

Additionally, Snow pursued personal studies and spent time discussing and answering gospel questions with fellow prisoners. Clawson recalled, "He was considered an excellent authority on doctrinal points, and his views were frequently sought; as we sat around the table during the long hours of the evening, he often discoursed interestingly upon matters pertaining to the past, present, and future conditions of man. I shall ever look back to those hours—hours passed in prison—as among the most profitable of my life."[106]

To be sure, Snow's presence brought comfort to others. Jens Hansen arrived in June 1886. He noted, "Was ushered in among the prisoners fresh fish was heard from all sides, which seems to be a common saying to when new prisoners arrive. The brethren greeted me very kindly and among them Apostle Lorenzo Snow and although the prison looks dark and gloomy I found myself among many of my friends—who all seemed to be cheerful and happy we had dry bread and black tea for supper."[107]

Sunday religious services rotated among various denominations. Latter-day Saints were able to meet on the first Sunday of the month. For example, on Sunday, July 4, 1886, Snow preached a special sermon entitled "Man's Inhumanity to Man."[108] On the following day, during the Fourth of July celebration, thieves stole some of his clothes.[109] Another special holiday was Thanksgiving 1886. The

Latter-day Saint women of Brigham City received permission from the warden to prepare a feast and program for all the prisoners in honor of Lorenzo Snow.[110] However, there was no special meal for Christmas a month later, a fact mentioned by some prisoners.

A few weeks later, Lorenzo Snow and several other Mormon prisoners had the unique opportunity to attend a program inside the warden's house. Clawson taught the warden's children, George and Florence Dow. Through his efforts, Snow and the others were invited to attend the 9:30 a.m. gathering outside the prison compound in the comforts of the "largest and best living room" in the warden's home.[111]

Another unusual experience that caught several Mormon diarists' attention was the day Lorenzo Snow asked the brethren to join him in a special ceremony. Clawson recalled, "Upon one occasion in the daytime, when the brethren had exclusive possession of the bunk room, President Lorenzo Snow made a startling and interesting announcement. He spoke to this effect: 'I propose, if it shall meet with the unanimous approval of all the brethren present, that we give the sacred shout. I realize that this is an extraordinary thing to do in a prison house. It has never been before, but inasmuch as we are incarcerated here for conscience sake, I'm sure we would be fully justified.'"[112]

Following the U.S. Supreme Court's decision to dismiss Snow's appeal, Caleb Walton West, the newly appointed Utah territorial governor, visited the prison on May 13, 1886, and held a lengthy interview with Snow. Adam Patterson, third district court of Utah reporter, made a transcription of the interview that appeared in local papers on the following day and then as a pamphlet.[113] Apparently, West hoped to convince Snow that continued resistance to federal law was futile. The governor promised to seek U.S. presidential pardons for all prisoners who pledged to obey the law. In the end, Snow and most of the other Latter-day Saints did not accept the offer because it meant they would have to abandon their wives, children, and grandchildren by cutting off all financial support and social relationships.

GOV. WEST AND THE POLYGAMISTS.

Report of His Interview with Apostle Lorenzo Snow, May 13, 1886, at the Utah Penitentiary.

His Proposals Rejected, and the Brethren Proclaim Their Defiance of the Law.

Following is a verified report of the visit of Governor Caleb W. West, of Utah, to the Utah Penitentiary, May 13th, 1886, wherein he states the purpose of his visit, and of the conversation which ensued between him and Apostle Lorenzo Snow; to which are appended three editorials relating to the subject, from THE SALT LAKE TRIBUNE of May 14th and 15th:

[From Salt Lake Tribune, May 14.]

Yesterday Governor West, accompanied by Secretary Thomas, Register Webb, Marshal Ireland, W. C. Hall, Esq., and Adam Patterson, the official reporter of the Third District Court, made a visit to the Utah Penitentiary. The object of the visit of the Governor was for the purpose of presenting to Lorenzo Snow and the other polygamists now in the Penitentiary the condition of affairs resulting from the late decison of the Supreme Court of the United States in the Snow case, and to say on behalf of Judge Zane and Prosecuting Attorney Dickson and himself, that if they would agree in good faith to obey the laws hereafter, they would recommend them to the clemency of President Cleveland.

The party left the Walker House at 1:30 p. m., and arrived at the Penitentiary at 2:30 p. m. Upon arriving there they were recieved by Warden Dow and conducted into one of the apartments of the building outside the wall. Apostle Lorenzo Snow, at the request of Governor West, was brought into the room, when the following conversation occurred between the Governor and Apostle Snow:

Governor West—Mr. Snow, I suppose you are advised of the action of the Supreme Court in your case?

Snow—Yes, sir; I have heard they have concluded they had no jurisdiction in my case.

Governor—Of course you are aware that that determination by that court makes final the decision of that case by the Supreme Court here.

Snow—I suppose so.

Governor—Under those circumstances, of course, that is now the law because it is the decision of the highest judicial tribunal to which it could be submitted, and I conceive that it would be a very opportune time to call and submit to you a proposition, which, in conjunction with Judge Zane and Mr. Dickson, we have thought advisable to make, in order to show you and the people of the Territory that they are mistaken in believing that those charged with the execution of the laws in the Territory are animated by any spirit of malice or vindictiveness toward the people who are in the majority in the Territory; that on the contrary their only wish and only desire; one which is nearest to their hearts, is to have the people of the Territory obey and respect the law. Upon consultation with Judge Zane and Mr. Dickson, and they supporting the view that I have suggested, I have come to say to you and your people here that we would unite in a

"Gov. West and the Polygamists" (1886), used by permission, L. Tom Perry Special Collections. Accounts of Governor Caleb W. West's visit to the penitentiary and his interview with Lorenzo Snow were published in local papers and as a pamphlet.

Lorenzo Snow believed his incarceration was a blessing in many ways. In particular, Snow had interviews with more than fifty "prominent men of the nation—such as educators, lawyers, ministers, politicians, and statesmen."[114] Snow, however, like other prisoners, sometimes felt he was on display for visitors. He noted, "It appears to be the practice to point me out to all visitors who secure passes to the Penitentiary as one of its principle curiosities on exhibition."[115] Nevertheless, in each case, Snow believed that he was able to answer questions about Mormonism and bear testimony of the Restoration. For example, Dr. J. L. Forwood, the mayor of Chester City, Pennsylvania, arrived at the penitentiary in August 1886.[116] Snow noted, "During the interview I bore a strong testimony and powerful testimony of the divine knowledge I had received concerning the restoration of the gifts and powers of the gospel, and the law of Celestial Marriage, and fixed resolve to adhere to our principles though at the cost of liberty and life."[117] Another important interview occurred on September 15, 1886, during the visit of Morrison R. Waite, chief justice of the U.S. Supreme Court.[118] He had issued the unanimous decision in the Reynolds case and would hear Snow's second appeal in a matter of months.[119] Because family visits to the prison were possible on only the first Thursday of the month and generally lasted only half an hour, these opportunities to meet with people on the outside brought relief from the daily monotony of incarceration.

LORENZO SNOW'S RELEASE

After completing the first six months of his sentence, Snow's attorneys filed for a writ of habeas corpus in the district court in Utah on October 22, 1886.[120] When the court refused, they appealed to the U.S. Supreme Court (Snow's second appeal to the Supreme Court) on November 22, 1886. Unlike the earlier appeal, the court agreed to consider Snow's case on November 24. On the following day, the *New York Times* reported, "In the matter of Lorenzo Snow, petitioner, appellant. Motion to advance granted and cause

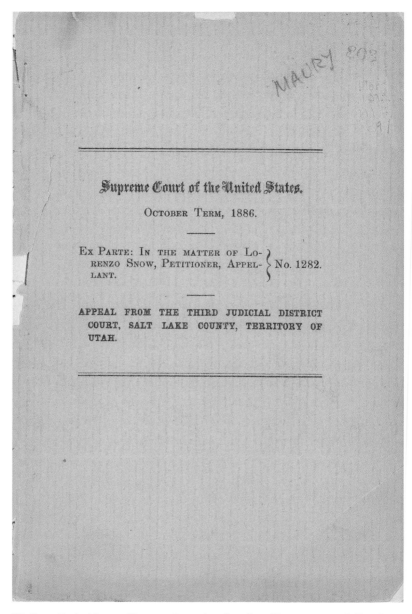

Supreme Court of the United States.

OCTOBER TERM, 1886.

EX PARTE: IN THE MATTER OF LO- ⎫
RENZO SNOW, PETITIONER, APPEL- ⎬ No. 1282.
LANT. ⎭

APPEAL FROM THE THIRD JUDICIAL DISTRICT
COURT, SALT LAKE COUNTY, TERRITORY OF
UTAH.

"Ex Parte: In the Matter of Lorenzo Snow, Appellant," used by permission, L. Tom Perry Special Collections. William Arden Maury, assistant attorney general of the United States, prepared written arguments that were submitted to the U.S. Supreme Court in Lorenzo Snow's first and second appeal in 1886.

assigned for argument on Jan. 17, at the calendar."[121] The purpose of this appeal was to challenge the constitutionality of Chief Justice Zane's segregation interpretation. In effect, Snow argued that being punished twice for the same crime violated his constitutional rights. Earlier, in a private communication received on June 1, 1886, Snow was informed by Franklin S. Richards that the segregation issue would come up in the autumn, and his lawyers expected the court's ruling to "be favorable to us."[122] Oral arguments were held on January 20, 1887, with Franklin S. Richards and George Ticknor Curtis representing the appellant. They "calculated that charging a single count for each day of the period, the logical extension of the government's theory, would result in an imprisonment of 547 years and fines amounting to $328,500."[123] The nation followed Snow's case, watching and waiting for the court's decision.[124] On February 7, 1887, the Supreme Court struck down the Utah District Court's earlier ruling, arguing that since cohabitation was by definition "a continuous offense, having duration," any attempt to divide it on temporal grounds into multiple indictments must be "wholly arbitrary" and therefore illegal.[125] This ruling ultimately saved hundreds of years of incarceration for Latter-day Saint prisoners. After years of major defeats and setbacks, this ruling represented a stunning victory for the Church.

Additionally, this legal success changed many Latter-day Saints' attitudes about life in hiding. Snow's attorney recalled, "Men who had been in hiding, because they were unwilling to incur the results of numerous prosecutions, came forward and pleaded guilty to one offence and paid the penalty. They were glad to terminate the trying condition of constant fear and apprehension, under which they had been obliged to live, and realized that after their terms of imprisonment expired they would come forth free men, without having made any promises." He added, "So numerous were they that the penitentiary was practically filled."[126]

Having already served his first six-month sentence as well as five months of his second sentence, Lorenzo Snow was released on

February 8, 1887, the day following the Supreme Court's ruling.[127] Snow's fellow prisoner Nicholas H. Groesbeck was released the same day as a result of the same ruling.[128] When he left the penitentiary, he, "like all the others, was offered a suit of clothes and $5, but he told the Government agent that he proposed to reverse the arrangement and donate that amount to the government as they would need it before they got through with the Mormon question."[129]

Lorenzo Snow reported upon his release, "Eleven months I had been incarcerated within the walls of a gloomy prison. Imagine for yourselves how like a dream it seemed when, suddenly and unexpectedly the prison gate flew open and clad in my striped convict suit, I was at once ushered into the presence of a multitude of warm-hearted friends, anxiously awaiting my appearance. O, what warm clasping and shaking of hands! What hearty greetings and experience of congratulations!"[130]

On February 13, 1887, the first Sunday of freedom, Lorenzo Snow spoke to the Saints in Salt Lake City. The *Deseret News* reported, "Apostle Lorenzo Snow addressed the congregation. . . . He read from Romans viii: 35 to 39: 'Who shall separate us from the love of Christ? Shall tribulation, or distress, or persecution, or famine, or nakedness, or peril, or sword? . . . For I am persuaded, that neither death, nor life, nor angels, nor principalities, nor powers, nor things present, nor things to come, Nor height, nor depth, nor any other creature, shall be able to separate us from the love of God, which is in Christ Jesus our Lord.'" The report continued, "He did not know how far along he had got in the scale of sacrifice, nor did any man. He never prayed to avoid sacrifice, but rather to be prepared to make it in the cause of truth. He did not want to go back to the penitentiary, but would go back a thousand times rather than disgrace that which God had given him."[131]

On March 8, 1887, a reporter summarized Lorenzo Snow's address in Brigham City: "In the prison [Snow] had much opportunity of doing good; many labors being there performed by him that could have been done nowhere else. He thanked God for it, and believed God would accept of his labors. He saw no one gloomy while he was there. Uncle Sam is not such a bad man. He has given us many good things. If he takes some of them away—why, we can only say 'Uncle Sam' giveth and 'Uncle Sam' taketh away. But his giving or taking is not going to hinder the work of God."[132]

In the following months, Lorenzo Snow's ministry continued beyond the prison. With other Church leaders still in hiding, Snow was asked to preside at general conference in the new Provo Tabernacle on April 6, 1887. Additionally, he spoke and presided at President John Taylor's funeral on July 29, 1887, in Salt Lake City. During this period, Lorenzo Snow held several late-night chats with Edward Bellamy about the Brigham City cooperative movement (the most successful cooperative association in Utah at the time). In 1888, Bellamy published his famous utopian novel, *Looking Backward: 2000–1887* (New York: William Tickner, 1888), the third bestselling book in nineteenth-century America behind *Uncle Tom's Cabin* and *Ben Hur*.

Though Lorenzo Snow's own prison experience ended in February 1887, persecution continued. On February 19, 1887, just ten days after Snow was released from the penitentiary, Congress passed a draconian law, the Edmunds-Tucker Act, further eroding Latter-day Saints' civil and property rights. It is impossible to determine what effect Snow's appeal and final victory had on passing the law, although Nathan B. Oman opined, "The success of Mormon lawyers in defeating overreaching prosecutorial theories" such as segregation and "the success of the Church leaders in evading arrest" forced the federal government to shift its strategy to "wider but less dramatic convictions."[133] Certainly, legislators had carefully watched Snow's appeal process, maybe even anticipating the final decision. They, along with federal officials in Utah, realized the Latter-day Saints had dramatically and successfully challenged their plans in the highest court of the land; however, they would not relent. Non-LDS attorney George Ticknor Curtis said he had never before witnessed such a rising storm, writing, "You are a mere handful of people; 150,000 against 50 or 60 million, and those millions have made up their minds that polygamy shall be exterminated *per fas et nefas* [Latin, 'completely']."[134]

Without the U.S. president's signature, the Edmunds-Tucker Act became law on March 3, 1887. This extreme measure required wives to testify against a husband, abolished the Nauvoo Legion (the territorial militia), dissolved the Perpetual Emigrating Fund Company in an effort to slow LDS emigration to the United States, disenfranchised women voters in the Utah Territory, initiated forfeiture proceedings against the Church, and allowed anyone to initiate charges of adultery against any individual (this had traditionally been reserved for legal spouses).

LORENZO SNOW'S PRISON WRITING

As noted, Lorenzo Snow maintained a lively correspondence with family members, friends, and acquaintances while in prison, thanking them for their support and offering them words of comfort and consolation during those trying times of the federal crusade. John Nicholson, who was incarcerated at the same time as Snow, observed that there were strict rules regarding writing and receiving letters at the Utah Territorial Penitentiary: "All correspondence, outgoing and incoming, is examined by the Warden. If, in his judgment, any communication contains aught objectionable, it is not permitted to go out. Letters, books, and periodicals, excepting local newspapers, can be received at any time. . . . Ordinarily convicts are permitted to write to friends on the outside twice a month, but oftener, by special permission, should some unusual emergency demand."[135] Additionally, contemporary sources indicate that the warden censored letters frequently and that the prisoners were aware of the practice and seem to have written knowing he would read what they said about him and their experience in prison.[136]

Lorenzo Snow wrote his first prison letter to family members two months after he began his sentence. In it he sardonically observed,

"In a general sense we are here as the invited guests of the Nation, boarded and lodged all at Government expense, a remarkable instance illustrating in a striking manner that spirit of philanthropy pervading the bosom of our mighty republic."[137] In what was apparently his last letter from prison to his family, he reflected on December 3, 1886, "I feel perfectly at home, and quite easy in my conscience, and feeling entirely foreign to those of a convict guilty of a crime."[138]

Additionally, Lorenzo Snow wrote several short, poetic, benedictory statements to various individuals—most likely for inclusion in their autograph albums—along with lengthier poems written to friends and family members. Some of these poems were published during his incarceration. For example, see "A Brother and Sister's Love," published in the *Deseret News* in 1886.[139]

RECORD BOOK DESCRIPTION

Lorenzo Snow kept copies of some of his prison writings in a small record book. Sporting a black leather cover imprinted with the word "RECORD," Lorenzo Snow's record book measures 19.5 × 12 centimeters and contains 224 lined pages. The cover and spine are damaged, but the pages are in excellent condition. In several places, someone (possibly Snow himself) corrected the text with gray and purple pencil (Lorenzo Snow preferred to use pencil); these corrections are noted in the footnotes.

The record book does not reflect the complete collection of his prison writing, as indicated by Orson F. Whitney's unpublished manuscript, "Later Leaves from the Life of Lorenzo Snow, President of the Twelve Apostles of the Church of Jesus Christ of Latter-day Saints. A Sequel to the Biography and Family Record of Lorenzo Snow" created in 1890, which includes numerous letters not included in the record book. Additionally, several poems written during his incarceration have been published and are not found in the record book.[140]

Fortunately for historians, the record book does contain poems and a few sentiments he received from others, including lengthy poems by his daughter Lydia and his sister Eliza R. Snow Smith. It also contains a poem by fellow prisoner Henry W. Naisbitt and Christmas and New Year's wishes from family members. Other entries include Helen E. Whitman's poem "The Mother's Altered Prayer" (pages [20]–[22]); a transcription of U.S. marshal Francis "Frank" H. Dyer's speech to prison inmates on August 23, 1886 (pages [23]–[24]); a poem by Rosena Bromley to her husband, William M. Bromley, a fellow prisoner with Lorenzo Snow, and the poetic reply Snow apparently wrote for William (pages [47]–[49]); a copy of a letter Rudger Clawson wrote to U.S. president Grover Cleveland (pages [74]–[75]); a copy of Lorenzo Snow's letter to Utah Congressional delegate John T. Caine asking him to see that Clawson's letter actually reach the president (page [73]); and a list of 150 men who had been committed to the Utah Penitentiary for "Polygamy and Unlawful Cohabitation" between November 3, 1884, and January 8, 1887, with each person's age, place of residence, length of sentence, amount of fine, date of imprisonment, and sentencing judge listed as well (pages [76]–[83]).

With the exception of Henry B. Naisbitt's poem (pages [50]–[53]), which is written in Naisbitt's own hand, the correspondence and copies described above (pages [5]–[83]) are in Rudger Clawson's hand. So too is the flyleaf inscription, "Lorenzo Snow Utah Penitentiary March 12th 1886."

Pages [84]–[99] (page [95] is blank) contain more copies of Lorenzo Snow's poetic correspondence but in his wife Minnie's hand; they were apparently copied into the record book sometime after Lorenzo Snow's release from prison. Minnie served as Lorenzo Snow's private secretary during his later life.[141] The first two of these latter poems are dated 1882; the remainder fall between June 1891 and March 1897 but do not appear in chronological order. Most are to family members, although one is to Susa Young Gates, including her nonpoetic reply (pages [86]–[90]), and another to "friends assembled to celebrate our Twentieth Wedding Anniversary" (page [94]).

One of the most interesting aspects of the record book is that it does not always reproduce the original item word for word. For example, Lorenzo Snow's poem to Marinda Goff, dated August 5, 1885, varies slightly between the entry in the autograph book and the copy found in the record book. In the autograph book the first three lines read:

While in a conversation with
Our holy Prophet Joseph Smith,
Just 'fore he shared a martyr's fate,

In the record book the first three lines read:

In private talk one evening with
Our Seer and Prophet Joseph Smith.
Before he shared a martyr's fate,

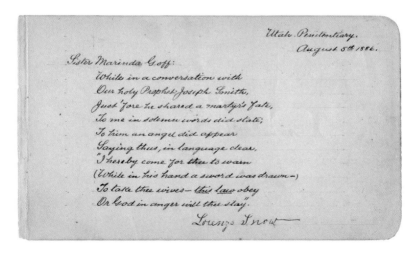

Marinda Goff's autograph album, highlighting Lorenzo Snow's entry, dated August 5, 1886, used by permission, David Bennion Judd, Orem, Utah.

The record book adds several lines not found in the original autograph book:

'Twas eighteen hundred forty three
This sacred law as shown to me
Which gives to man his loving wives
God's only path to endless lives

Additionally, it is interesting to note that the main body of the text in the autograph book is recorded in the handwriting of Rudger Clawson. However, Lorenzo Snow added his distinctive signature with his own hand.[142]

SIGNIFICANCE OF THE RECORD BOOK

Prison provided Lorenzo Snow an opportunity to pray, reflect, converse, and document his feelings and thoughts through the written word. He highlights the paradox of his incarceration, where personal tragedy was expected to eventually turn into divine vindication. His prison writings draw attention to another paradox: although he was imprisoned, his words escaped from within the prison walls to be shared with the outside world, including a Charles W. Carter photograph montage printed in 1886.

There are several additional significances to the record book. First, because many of the entries are copies of letters and poems he wrote to friends and family members, the record book sheds some much-needed light on the thoughts, personality, and personal life of Lorenzo Snow—one of the least studied and most poorly understood and appreciated of our modern prophets. His vocabulary, his humor, his compassion, and the deftness with which he puts his thoughts into verse all reveal facets of Lorenzo Snow's intellect and character unfamiliar to many Church members today.

Second, the record book is significant for its doctrinal content, particularly Lorenzo Snow's teachings concerning the pre-earth life. Writing to comfort the families of those serving prison time with him, Lorenzo Snow repeatedly asserts that these men had agreed before coming to earth to uphold the teachings of the prophets regarding plural marriage and, if necessary, go to jail

Lorenzo Snow montage, 1886, by Charles W. Carter, used by permission, Church History Library. Carter, a well-known Salt Lake City photographer, produced a cabinet card (4″ × 6″) size photograph entitled "Mutual Affection" in 1886. This collage included portraits of Lorenzo Snow and his sister, Eliza R. Snow Smith; a poem by Lorenzo to Eliza (dated September 29, 1886); her poetic response (dated October 7, 1886) originally published in the *Deseret News*; and a photograph of the Utah Territorial Penitentiary in the lower left-hand corner. Lorenzo Snow's poem to his sister and her response appear in his record book. See pages 43–44, 50–52.

rather than renounce those beliefs (see pages [8], [38]–[39]). Time and again, he refers to their prison sentence as a "mission" to which they had committed themselves previously, thereby providing us with glimpses into the eternal context of this world's experiences. Other topics he addresses include children (see pages [12], [84]), the promise of future glory for remaining faithful in tribulation (see pages [13], [19], [25], [87]–[88]), the origin of plural marriage in the latter days (see page [16]), and the potential for man to become like God (see pages [26]–[27], [46], [90]–[92]).

Finally, Lorenzo Snow's record book is an important primary source for students of the federal antipolygamy crusade. Personal and thoughtful, Lorenzo Snow's poems and letters written within prison walls are invaluable for understanding how the Saints viewed their persecutions (see pages [7], [41], [56], [63]–[66]), justified their resistance to the laws (see pages [10]–[11], [57]), and found the will to carry on despite increasingly difficult circumstances (see pages [67], [69]). Writing as both a prisoner and an Apostle, Lorenzo Snow provides us with a unique viewpoint on the dark days of the 1880s.

Utah Penitentiary, May 30, 1887, photograph by Charles R. Savage, used by permission, Church History Library. This photograph shows the entrance to the prison and the warden's home looking east.

EDITORIAL PROCEDURES

We have transcribed the record book's entries with as little editing as possible. Original capitalization, punctuation, spelling, superscripts, underlining, and paragraphing have been retained, although underlined superscripts have not been underlined here. Lines dividing stanzas in various poems have been retained, and heavier, darker handwriting has been rendered in **bold** type. Strikeouts have been indicated as words with a line drawn through the center. Square brackets [ ] have been used to set off editorial clarifications, while angle brackets < > have been used to indicate textual insertions made by the original writers. Dates were often written with a heavy double comma following the day (e.g., Sept. 6,, 1886); these have been transcribed with one comma. Double dashes have been rendered with a single dash. The appendix lists the individuals mentioned in the record book that could be identified. Where we could not narrow an individual to a specific person, we have omitted the individual's information.

NOTES

1. Ioan Davies, *Writers in Prison* (Cambridge, MA: Basil Backwell, 1990), 3.
2. See, for example, H. Bruce Franklin, *American Prisoners and Ex-Prisoners: Their Writings, An Annotated Bibliography of Published Works, 1798–1981* (Westport, CT: Lawrence Hill & Company, 1982).
3. Alvare De Silva, ed., *The Last Letters of Thomas More* (Grand Rapids, MI: Eerdmans, 2000); Dietrich Bonhoffer, *Letters and Papers from Prison* (New York: Touchstone, 1997); and Martin Luther King Jr., *Why We Can't Wait* (New York: New American Library, 2000).
4. W. Clark Gilpin, "The Letter from Prison in Christian History and Theology," *The Religion & Culture Web Forum*, January 2003, 1.
5. Gilpin, "The Letter from Prison," 1.
6. See Dean C. Jessee, ed., *Personal Writings of Joseph Smith* (Salt Lake City: Deseret Book; Provo, UT: Brigham Young University Press, 2002), 620–35.
7. A brief introduction to the beginnings of plural marriage is found in Glen M. Leonard, *Nauvoo: A Place of Peace, A People of Promise* (Salt Lake City: Deseret Book and Provo, UT: and Brigham Young University Press, 2002), 341–56.
8. Sarah Barringer Gordon, *The Mormon Question: Polygamy and Constitutional Conflict in Nineteenth Century America* (Chapel Hill: The University of North Carolina Press, 2002), 142.
9. For a general view of how Latter-day Saints were depicted for the period from 1869 through 1890, see Gary L. Bunker and Davis Bitton, *The Mormon Graphic Image,*

1834–1914: Cartoons, Caricatures, and Illustration (Salt Lake City: University of Utah Press, 1983), 33–56.

10. Gordon, *The Mormon Question*, 85.
11. Gordon, *The Mormon Question*, 87.
12. Thomas G. Alexander, *Utah: The Right Place* (Salt Lake City: Gibbs Smith, 2003), 192.
13. Nathan B. Oman, "The Story of a Forgotten Battle: Reviewing *The Mormon Question: Polygamy and Constitutional Conflict in Nineteenth-Century America*," *Brigham Young University Law Review* 3 (2002): 747.
14. Gordon, *The Mormon Question*, 155–56.
15. Kathryn M. Daynes, *More Wives Than One: Transformation of the Mormon Marriage System, 1840–1910* (Urbana and Chicago: University of Illinois Press, 2001), 175.
16. Oman, "The Story of a Forgotten Battle," 750.
17. Thomas G. Alexander to Richard Neitzel Holzapfel, March 22, 2010, in author's possession.
18. See Ann Eliza Young, *Wife No. 19* (Hartford: Dustin, Gilman & Co., 1875); T. B. H. Stenhouse, *Exposé of Polygamy: A Lady's Life among the Mormons* (New York: American News Company, 1872); and T. B. H. Stenhouse, *Tell It All: The Story of a Life's Experience in Mormonism*, (Hartford, CT: A. D. Worthington, 1877).
19. John Gary Maxwell, "Ann Eliza's Next Best Friend," in *Gettysburg to Great Salt Lake: George R. Maxwell, Civil War Hero and Federal Marshal among the Mormons* (Norman, OK: Arthur H. Clark, 2010), 181.
20. B. Carmon Hardy, *Solemn Covenant: The Mormon Polygamous Passage* (Urbana: University of Illinois Press, 1992), 39–83.
21. See Edwin Brown Firmage and Richard Collin Mangrum, *Zion in the Courts: A Legal History of the Church of Jesus Christ of Latter-day Saints, 1830–1900* (Urbana: University of Illinois Press, 1988), 160–260.
22. Gordon, *The Mormon Question*, 81.
23. Firmage and Mangrum, *Zion in the Courts*, 131.
24. Firmage and Mangrum, *Zion in the Courts*, 140–41.
25. Firmage and Mangrum, *Zion in the Courts*, 148.
26. Firmage and Mangrum, *Zion in the Courts*, 148–49.
27. See Bruce Van Orden, *The Life of George Reynolds: Prisoner for Conscience' Sake* (Salt Lake City: Deseret Book, 1992), 58–100.
28. Oman, "The Story of a Forgotten Battle," 752.
29. Oman, "The Story of a Forgotten Battle," 752.
30. Noah Feldman, *Divided by God: America's Church-State Problem* (New York: Farrar, Straus and Giroux, 2005), 101.
31. Firmage and Mangrum, *Zion in the Courts*, 151–59.
32. Oman, "The Story of a Forgotten Battle," 751.
33. Edward Leo Lyman, *Political Deliverance: The Mormon Quest for Utah Statehood* (Urbana: University of Illinois Press, 1986), 22–23.
34. Lyman, *Political Deliverance*, 23.
35. Firmage and Mangrum, *Zion in the Courts*, 149.
36. Firmage and Mangrum, *Zion in the Courts*, 171.
37. Firmage and Mangrum, *Zion in the Courts*, 167–79.
38. Daynes, *More Wives Than One*, 183.
39. Rosa Mae M. Evans argued that judges Charles S. Zane and Jacob S. Boreman often sentenced Latter-day Saints to the maximum penalties allowed by the law while non–Latter-day Saints were sentenced to much less severe penalties for the same offense. See Rosa Mae M. Evans, "Judicial Prosecution of Prisoners for LDS Plural

Marriage Prison Sentences, 1884–1895" (master's thesis, Brigham Young University, 1986), 41.

40. Lyman, *Political Deliverance*, 24–25; see also Thomas G. Alexander, "Charles S. Zane: Apostle of the New Era," *Utah Historical Quarterly* 34, no. 4 (Fall 1966): 290–319.

41. Lyman, *Political Deliverance*, 25.

42. Lyman, *Political Deliverance*, 25.

43. Ken Driggs, "Lorenzo Snow's Appellate Court Victory," *Utah Historical Quarterly* 58, no. 1 (Winter 1990): 87.

44. Oman, "The Story of a Forgotten Battle," 748–49.

45. See for example, Charles Lowell Walker's poem, dated May 17, 1885, "There's an under-ground Railroad. Evading the Bailroad. Which ne'er was a Jailroad, In Utah," in A. Karl Larson and Katharine Miles Larson, eds., *Diary of Charles Lowell Walker* (Logan: Utah State University Press, 1980), 2:647.

46. For a brief history of the Mormon Underground, see James B. Allen and Glen M. Leonard, *The Story of the Latter-day Saints*, 2nd ed. rev. (Salt Lake City: Deseret Book, 1992), 399–407.

47. T. Edgar Lyon, review of *The "Americanization" of Utah for Statehood*, by Gustive O. Larson, *BYU Studies* 12, no. 1 (Autumn 1971): 139.

48. National newspapers acknowledged the problem and asked for stricter laws and enforcement. See, for example, "One Year of the Edmunds Law," *The New York Times*, January 3, 1886, 7.

49. For a review of women's experience on the Underground, see Kimberly J. James, "'Between Two Fires': Women on the 'Underground' of Mormon Polygamy," *Journal of Mormon History* 8 (1981): 49–61.

50. Leonard J. Arrington and Davis Bitton, *The Mormon Experience: A History of the Latter-day Saints* (New York: Alfred A. Knopf, 1979), 181.

51. Lyman, *Political Deliverance*, 25.

52. Stan Larson, *A Ministry of Meetings: The Apostolic Diaries of Rudger Clawson* (Salt Lake City: Signature Books, 1993), x.

53. Ironically, Clawson's first wife divorced him in July 1885 during his incarceration, leaving him with only one wife. See Stan Larson, ed., *Prisoner for Polygamy: The Memoirs and Letters of Rudger Clawson at the Utah Territorial Penitentiary, 1884–87* (Urbana: University of Illinois Press, 1993), 8.

54. See Table 3.2, "Conviction for Polygamy and Unlawful Cohabitation in Utah Territory," in Stephen Cresswell, *Mormons and Cowboys, Moonshiners and Klansmen: Federal Law Enforcement in the South and West, 1870–1893* (Tuscaloosa: University of Alabama Press, 1991), 100.

55. For a brief biographical review of his life, see Clyde J. Williams, "Lorenzo Snow," in *Encyclopedia of Latter-day Saint History*, ed. Arnold K. Garr, Donald Q. Cannon, and Richard O. Cowan (Salt Lake City: Deseret Book, 2000), 1151–54, and Heidi S. Swinton, "Lorenzo Snow," in *The Presidents of the Church*, ed. Leonard J. Arrington (Salt Lake City: Deseret Book, 1986), 144–76. For a more comprehensive account, see Thomas C. Romney, *The Life of Lorenzo Snow: Fifth President of the Church of Jesus Christ of Latter-day Saints* (Salt Lake City: S.U.P Memorial Foundation, 1955).

56. These dates are based on family group records, Family Search Ancestral File, and Lisle G. Brown, comp., *Nauvoo Sealings, Adoptions, and Anointings: A Comprehensive Register of Persons Receiving LDS Temple Ordinances, 1841–1846* (Salt Lake City: Smith-Pettit Foundation, 2006), 290–91. Another reconstruction is found in George D. Smith, *Nauvoo Polygamy* (Salt Lake City: Signature Books, 2008), 256–57.

57. Richard S. Van Wagoner and Steven C. Walker, *A Book of Mormons* (Salt Lake City: Signature Press, 1982), 333.

58. Lorenzo and Mary Elizabeth Houtz Snow's first child, Lydia May Snow, was born on January 21, 1860, so the marriage must have taken place sometime before the spring of 1859.

59. Abraham H. Cannon Journal, April 5, 1894, L. Tom Perry Special Collections, Harold B. Lee Library, Brigham Young University, Provo, Utah; see also D. Michael Quinn, "LDS Church Authority and New Plural Marriages, 1890–1904," *Dialogue: A Journal of Mormon Thought* 18, no. 1 (Spring 1985): 66n222.

60. At his seventieth birthday celebration in 1884, more than one hundred family members celebrated in Brigham City. See Snow, *Biography and Family Record*, 461. Lorenzo eventually fathered forty-two children and raised another three children from Mary Adaline Goddard's previous marriage to George Washington Hendrickson, so Lorenzo's family consisted of forty-five children.

61. See Lowell C. Bennion, Alan L. Morrell, and Thomas Charter, *Polygamy in Lorenzo Snow's Brigham City: An Architectural Tour* (Salt Lake City: University of Utah Press, 2005), 33.

62. Lorenzo Snow, "Discourse by Apostle Lorenzo Snow," in *Journal of Discourses* (London: Latter-day Saints' Books Depot, 1886) 26:365.

63. "Lorenzo Snow Family Papers: Notes by LeRoi C. Snow, ca. 1890," May 1885, L. Tom Perry Special Collections, Harold B. Lee Library, Brigham Young University, Provo, UT.

64. "Lorenzo Snow Family Papers," July 1885.

65. First Presidency to Lorenzo Snow, July 5, 1885, in Romney, *The Life of Lorenzo Snow*, 355–56; "Lorenzo Snow Family Papers," July 2, 1885.

66. "Lorenzo Snow Family Papers," September 24, 1885.

67. Oman, "The Story of a Forgotten Battle," 749.

68. See 120 U.S. 274, 7 S. Ct. 556.

69. M. Koch, *His Ten Wives: The Travels, Trial and Conviction of the Mormon Apostle, Lorenzo Snow* (Butte, MT: Miner Publishing, 1887), 10.

70. "Lorenzo Snow Family Papers," November 20, 1885.

71. "Lorenzo Snow Arraigned," *Deseret News*, December 16, 1885, 760.

72. "First District Court," *Deseret News*, January 13, 1886, 818.

73. Hardy, *Solemn Covenant*, 50–51. For a review of the revelations President John Taylor received at this time, see Richard Neitzel Holzapfel and Christopher C. Jones, "'John the Revelator': The Written Revelations of John Taylor," in *Champion of Liberty: John Taylor*, ed. Mary Jane Woodger (Provo, UT: Religious Studies Center, Brigham Young University; Salt Lake City: Deseret Book, 2009), 273–308.

74. Daynes, *More Wives Than One*, 183.

75. "Lorenzo Snow Family Papers," January 5, 1886.

76. "Apostle Snow Convicted," *New York Times*, January 1, 1886, 1.

77. Driggs, "Lorenzo Snow's Appellate Court Victory," 85.

78. "Lorenzo Snow Family Papers," January 5, 1886.

79. "Apostle Snow Convicted," *New York Times*, January 6, 1886, 2.

80. Snow, in *Journal of Discourses*, 365–66.

81. Snow, in *Journal of Discourses*, 368.

82. Charles Lowell Walker Diary, January 8, 1886, as cited in Larson and Larson, *Diary of Charles Lowell Walker*, 2:660–61.

83. Firmage and Mangrum, *Zion in the Courts*, 179.

84. "A Surprise," *Deseret Evening News*, January 20, 1886, 2.

85. Firmage and Mangrum, *Zion in the Courts*, 179. Later, Congress attempted to rectify the problem by appointing an additional justice so that the justice who had tried the case in district court could be disqualified during an appeal.
86. *United States v. Snow*, 9 P. at 503 and 505.
87. *United States v. Snow*, 9 P. at 687-688.
88. *United States v. Snow*, 9 P. 697, 698
89. Lorenzo Snow to Franklin S. Richard, March 1, 1886, L. Tom Perry Special Collections.
90. List of Prisoners in the Utah Penitentiary, 213, Utah State Historical Society.
91. Cannon Journal, March 12, 1886.
92. John D. Cornham and J. P. Allen to Warden, Utah Penitentiary, January 16, 1886, as cited in Orson F. Whitney, "Later Leaves from the Life of Lorenzo Snow, President of the Twelve Apostles of the Church of Jesus Christ of Latter-day Saints. A Sequel to the Biography and Family Record of Lorenzo Snow," 177, L. Tom Perry Special Collections.
93. Whitney, "Later Leaves," 177.
94. For a general overview of prison life for Latter-day Saints, see Melvin Bashore, "Life behind Bars: Mormon Cohabs of the 1880s," *Utah Historical Quarterly* 47 (Winter 1970): 22–41.
95. John Nicholson, *The Martyrdom of Joseph Standing* (Salt Lake City: Deseret News, 1886), 96.
96. Cannon Journal, March 19, 1886.
97. Cannon Journal, March 17, 1886.
98. Cannon Journal, March 17, 1886.
99. Larson, *Prisoner for Polygamy*, 103.
100. "My Boudoir," *Juvenile Instructor*, February 1, 1887, 43. LeRoi Snow attributes this poem to his father; see "Lorenzo Snow Family Papers," February 1, 1887. The inclusion in the record book seems to confirm Snow's authorship.
101. Cannon Journal, May 10, 1886.
102. James Moyle noted, "Brother Snow is not as well as I would like to see [him]. You never hear him murmur or complain," James Moyle Diary, April 3, 1886, Church History Library, Salt Lake City, Utah. Cannon also mentions Snow's cold and headache; see Cannon Journal, March 25, 1886.
103. Lorenzo Snow to Family, June 13, 1886; as cited in Whitney, "Later Leaves," 247.
104. Jens Hansen Diary, June 4, 1886, L. Tom Perry Special Collections.
105. "The Penitentiary School," *Utah Journal*, July 14, 1886, [1].
106. Larson, *Prisoner for Polygamy*, 128.
107. Hansen Diary, June 2, 1886.
108. Whitney, "Later Leaves," 234.
109. Cannon Journal, July 5, 1886.
110. *Deseret News*, December 1, 1886, 733.
111. Larsen, *Prisoner for Polygamy*, 100.
112. Larson, *Prisoner for Polygamy*, 105.
113. *Gov. West and the Polygamists: Report of His Interview with Apostle Lorenzo Snow, May 13, 1886* (Salt Lake City: Salt Lake Tribune, 1886).
114. Whitney, "Later Leaves," 301, see also Lorenzo Snow, "How I Gained My Testimony," *Young Woman's Journal*, February 1893, 214.
115. Lorenzo Snow to Family, September 29, 1886, as cited in Snow, "How I Gained My Testimony," 214.
116. The local Chester, Pennsylvania newspaper reported, "His visit in Salt Lake City was one of the most pleasant of the entire trip, as friends did everything to make his stay

pleasant and profitable," *Chester Evening Times*, August 31, 1886, 3. We may assume that one of the reasons it was "profitable" was because of his visit with Lorenzo Snow.

117. Lorenzo Snow to Family, August 24, 1886, as cited in Whitney, "Later Leaves," 261.
118. "Lorenzo Snow Family Papers," September 15, 1886.
119. See Lyman, *Political Deliverance*, 21.
120. "Lorenzo Snow Family Papers," October 22, 1886.
121. "United States Supreme Court," *New York Times*, November 25, 1886, 3.
122. Cannon Diary, June 1, 1886.
123. Driggs, "Lorenzo Snow's Appellate Court Victory," 89.
124. See for example "A Mormon's Imprisonment," *New York Times*, January 21, 1887, 3.
125. "Reversed!" *Deseret Evening News*, February 7, 1887, 3.
126. Franklin S. Richards, "Address Delivered by President Franklin S. Richard to the High Priests Quorum of Ensign Stake," November 13, 1932, 14, Church History Library.
127. Romney, *Lorenzo Snow*, 365.
128. "Lorenzo Snow Family Papers," February 8, 1887.
129. Whitney, "Later Leaves," 301.
130. Whitney, "Later Leaves," 287–88.
131. "Sunday Services," *Deseret News*, February 13, 1887, 3.
132. Whitney, "Later Leaves," 301.
133. Oman, "The Story of a Forgotten Battle," 748–49.
134. George Ticknor Curtis to Franklin S. Richards, January 23, 1887, Church History Library.
135. Nicholson, *The Martyrdom of Joseph Standing*, 100.
136. See for example, George Brown Bailey to Elsie and Children, July 25, 1886, as cited in Gary E. Stay, comp., "The Internments of George Brown Bailey in the Utah Penitentiary 1886 and 1889," [10–13], L. Tom Perry Special Collections.
137. Lorenzo Snow to Family, May 4, 1886, as cited in Whitney, "Later Leaves," 178.
138. Lorenzo Snow to Family, December 3, 1886, as cited in Whitney, "Later Leaves," 271.
139. *Deseret News*, November 3, 1886, 658; see also Jill Mulvay Derr and Karen Lynn Davidson, eds., *Eliza R. Snow: The Complete Poetry* (Salt Lake City: Deseret News; Provo: Brigham Young University Press, 2009), 1027–30, 1267–68.
140. See, for example, Lillie Freeze, "Mrs. Minnie J. Snow," *Young Woman's Journal*, May 1891, 345.
141. Freeze, "Mrs. Minnie J. Snow," 344.
142. Lorenzo Snow to Marinda Goff, August 5, 1886, Marinda Goff Autograph Album, in private possession, copy in the L. Tom Perry Special Collections.

Transcript of Lorenzo Snow's Record Book

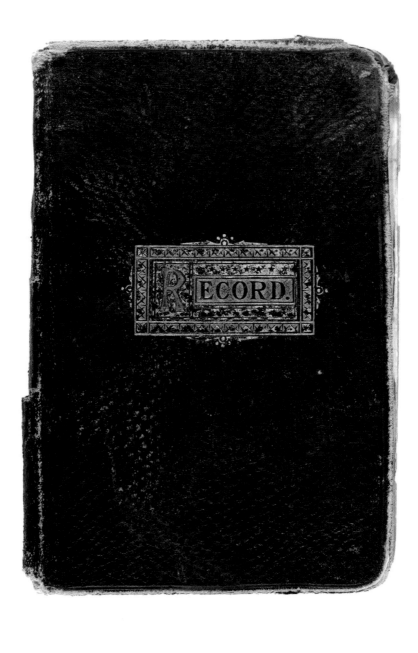

Record.[1]

Lorenzo Snow
Utah Penitentiary
March 12th 1886[2]

---

1. This is found on the volume's outside cover, in gold and black, with a gold and white border (see image opposite).
2. These three lines are on the volume's unlined flyleaf (see image on next page).

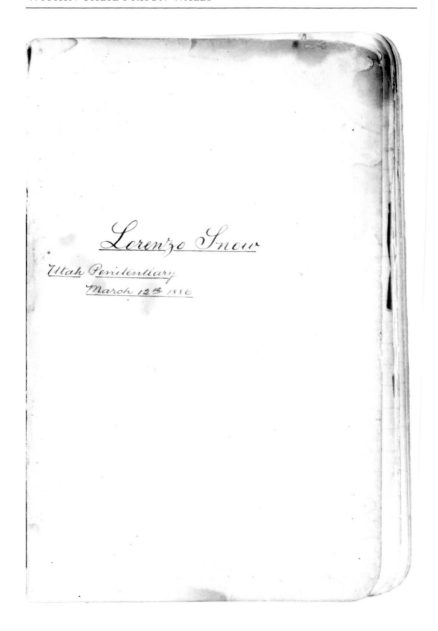

[1–4]

[Blank]

[5]

Copies   Utah Penitentiary

June 5th 1886

Sister Edna Lambert

May there be but little bitterness in thy innocent and happy life but may there ever spring in its eternal round fragrant flowers bright and beautifull

Lorenzo Snow.

Utah Penitentiary

June 8th 1886

Sister Alice Cannon

God hath made thee a beautiful Queen and given thee a Kingdom; thou thyself art that Kingdom; govern wisely Sister Alice and God will enlarge and exalt thee and thy Kingdom in this life, and in the life celestial, enlarge beautify <and glorify> thee and it through countless ages.

Lorenzo Snow.

Utah Penitentiary

Bro S. F. [Ball]   June 8th 1886

Sacrifice and obedience bring forth honor and immortality.

Lorenzo Snow.

[6]

Utah Penitentiary
June 23rd 1886

Brother Burningham:
   Pleasant tricks thou oft hast played,
   And teased thy friends in playfull mood;
   But as therefor they back have paid
   That what they owed, all wish thee good,
   And nevermore, Dear Burningham,
   Thou here be forced by "Uncle Sam".

Lorenzo Snow.

Utah Penitentiary
June 23rd 1886

Brother Bowen:
   A talent rare to thee is given
   For music sweet—a gift of Heaven:
   With easy grace and science true
   Thy Choir is taught, and strictly too,
   And thou with them much joy hast given
   To all thy friends whil'st here in prison.

Lorenzo Snow.

[7]
Utah Penitentiary
July 24th 1886

Brother Charles Denney:
 As we behold thy cheerfull face,
 No sorrow see—no tears we trace;
 And seest thou art never sad,
 It gives us joy—our hearts are glad
 To find thee so when here confined
 By Law illegally defined.
 And if thy bonds thou'dt still disdain
 In word, in heart, will n'er complain,
 When time grows old 'twill then be found
 It's added brightness to thy crown.

Lorenzo Snow.

Utah Penitentiary
June 10th 1886

Brother W. G. Bickley
 Thy anxious wish to gratify
 My autograph I here bestow,
 And give beside, Dear Friend, hereby
 My kind regards,—Lorenzo Snow.

7

[8]

Utah Penitentiary
July 26th 1886

Brother Herbert J. Foulger:
    Away in yonder realms above
    Where dwells our God who rules by love
    Some future day you'll surely find
    'Twas there thou hadst this call divine
    To show to man, and Gods on high
    Thy loving wives thou'dst not deny,
    Nor let thy heart by danger pall
    Through fiercest threats of prison walls.

Lorenzo Snow.

Utah Penitentiary
June 10th 1886

Sister Maria Goff:
    To Hyrum Goff a mission's given
    To dwell within these prison walls,
    And thou, his wife, 'twill please high heaven
    For thee to glory in this call.

Lorenzo Snow

[9]

Utah Penitentiary

July 27th 1886

Mrs Mina Cannon:

When thou didst live in realms above
Where dwells our God supreme in love,
Did'st not thou then with Him agree
To come to Earth a wife to be;
Help make thy lord a happy life
Be wise, be true, a loving wife?
When from thy mind the veil is riven,
Things now past are shown in vision,
Then happy truths by thee'll be found
To make thy heart with joy abound.

Lorenzo Snow.

[10]

Utah Penitentiary
July 29th 1886

Mrs Lydia Snow Pierce:
    With anxious wish thy heart to cheer
    I pen these lines, My Daughter Dear,
    As feeling sure 'tw'od never do
    To leave unanswered letter two,[3]
    So nice, so kind, so very good
    I'd write just like it if I could.
    Please answer this the same in kind
    As suits the best, in prose or rhyme.
        I feel content and happy too
        In that my Master's work I do
        In coming here within these walls
        To help, to cheer, and comfort all.
    Away, aloft in realms above
    Where dwells our God supreme in love,
    Where truth and light forever shine,
    I had, no doubt, a call divine
    To show to man, and Gods on high
    My wives I never would deny,
    Nor heart beside should never pall
    By fiercest threats of prison walls.

---

3.   The phrase "letter two" is underlined in purple pencil.

[11]

Away in yonder spirit land,
No doubt, we there did lift our hand,
Approving what was then proposed
To do on Earth what since we've show'd
Resolve to do—the work of God,
Nor choose ourselves the manner how,[4]
But to <u>His</u> <u>wish</u> in silence bow.
Could we escape in every form
Summer's heat, and winter's storm,
And walk o'er paths delightsome fair
And do Gods work with careless care,
Of course t'would be some pleasure rare,
But where's our glory—what's <u>our</u> share?
In former days, and modern too
With blood and pillage had to do
God's holy people—suffer . . . death;
For thus the holy scripture saith—
"In all things here will thee I prove[5]
E'n unto death—it me behoves".
We need not fear this cost to weigh
For soon will 'rise that glor'us day
When those who there are faithfull found
As Gods on high will then be crowned.

(over)

---

4. The word "how" is underlined in purple pencil.
5. The word "I" has been changed in purple pencil to "I'll."

[12]

O, Daughter Dear, thyself should know,
Improve each day, and wiser grow,
Be gentle, meek, in heart and mind
And shun each wrong of every kind
God's Spirit mind—ever to it bow,
Then sure as Sun doth rise, or water's flow
In world celestial Thee I'll see
A Godess crowned—Celestial Queen.

Affectionately
Your Father
Lorenzo Snow

Utah Penitentiary

July 31ˢᵗ 1886

Brother J. P. Ball:

In U.S. Courts 'twas nobly shown
Thy loving wives thou'dst not disown,
And hence, My Friend, Dear Brother Ball
You're here confined in prison walls.
So having honor'd God thus well
On thee judicial wrath has fell.
While here thou'st spent a placid life,
No temper shown to kindle strife,
But always seen in pleasant mood,
And always gentle, kind and good.
As told above, beloved friend,
This ever do—the truth defend;
Then highest life that Gods bestow
To thee and wives, will ever flow.

Lorenzo Snow.

[14]

Utah Penitentiary
Aug 3rd 1886

Sister Leonora Cannon:
May He who dwells in realms above
Oft' strew thy path with roses bright,
Enfold thee in his arms of love,
Thy mind with wisest thoughts indite.[6]

Lorenzo Snow

Utah Penitentiary
Aug 4th 1886

Mrs Clarissa Snow McAllister:
  Dear Daughter:
Amid these gloomy walls confined
Sweet thoughts of thee oft', come to mind
Of love and kindness ever shown
From childhood up to woman grown.
  Thou'st truly made a record clear
  No vital wrong doth there appear.
  Life's flowing stream since thou wast born
  Has borne thee gently, proudly on
  E'en to the present, and 'twill do
  E'en to the end so bear thee through[7]

---

6. The word "indite" is in darker ink in another hand.
7. The word "through" is followed by a period in gray pencil.

14

Utah Penitentiary
Aug 3rd 1886

Sister Leonora Cannon:

May He who dwells in realms above
Oft strew thy path with roses bright;
Enfold thee in his arms of love,
Thy mind with wisest thoughts indite.

Lorenzo Snow

Utah Penitentiary
Aug 4th 1886

Mrs Clarissa Snow McAllister:

Dear Daughter:

Amid these gloomy walls confined
Sweet thoughts of thee oft come to mind
Of love and Kindness ever shown
From childhood up to woman grown.

Thou'st truly made a record clear
No vital wrong doth there appear.
Life's flowing stream since thou wast born
Has borne thee gently, proudly on
E'en to the present, and 'twill do
E'en to the end so bear thee through.

WITHIN THESE PRISON WALLS

15

From One to Many thou hadst grown
And Queen thou reignest o'er thy own
Sweet Kingdom:- Though here its birth,
Began in time, on Mother Earth,
To brighter realms 'twill wing its way
Majestic march through endless day.
    Now listen, please, my Daughter Dear,
    What father saith:- indulge no fear;
    Thy care be only still endure,
    Thy duty do - thy crown is sure.
In worlds Celestial thou wilt find
From Kingdom thine, and offspring thine
Most joy and bliss thou'lt there derive
Which right no one can thee deprive.
    Then let thy heart in quiet rest
    What God doth dictate that is best
    To me, to you, to all concerned
    And none can have but what she's earned.
            Affectionately Your Father
                Lorenzo Snow,

16

[15]

From <u>One</u> <u>to</u> <u>Many</u> thou hast grown
And Queen thou reignest o'er thy own
Sweet Kingdom:—Though <u>here</u> its birth,[8]
Began in time, on Mother Earth,
To brighter realms 'twill wing its way
Majestic march through endless day.
    Now listen, please, my Daughter Dear,
    What father saith:—indulge no fear;
    Thy care be only still endure,
    Thy duty do—thy crown is sure.
In worlds Celestial thou wilt find
From kingdom thine, and offspring thine
Most joy and bliss thou'lt there derive
Which right no one can thee deprive.
    Then let thy heart in quiet rest
    What God doth dictate that is best
    To me, to you, to all concerned
    And none can have but what she's earned.
Affectionately Your Father
Lorenzo Snow.

---

8. The word "yet" is inserted in purple pencil between "Though" and "here."

[16]

Utah Penitentiary.
Aug 5th 1886.

Sister Marinda Goff:
In private talk one evening with
Our Seer and Prophet Joseph Smith,[9]
Before he shared a martyr's fate,
To me in solemn words did state:
To him an angel did appear
Saying thus, in language clear,
"I hereby come for thee to warn
(While in his hand a sword was drawn—)
To take thee wives—this law obey
Or God in anger will thee slay".[10]
'Twas eighteen hundred forty three
This sacred law was shown to me
Which gives to man his loving wives
God's only path to endless lives.[11]

Lorenzo Snow.

---

9. "In private . . . Prophet Jo" is in gray pencil in another hand.
10. According to an affidavit Snow made in Brigham City on August 28, 1869, this visit with Joseph, during which Joseph related his experience with the angel and the drawn sword, took place in April 1843, shortly after Snow's return from England. Joseph had asked Snow to accompany him on a walk, which he did. Sitting down on a large log near the bank of the Mississippi River, Joseph reportedly told Snow that "the Lord had revealed it [plural marriage] unto him and commanded him to have women sealed to him as wives, that he [Joseph] foresaw the trouble that would follow and sought to turn away from the commandment, that an angel from heaven appeared before him with a drawn sword, threatening him with destruction unless he went forward and obeyed the commandment." See "Apostle Lorenzo Snow's Testimony," in Andrew Jenson, ed., *Historical Record* 6 (1887), 222. Other firsthand accounts of Joseph relating the story of the angel with the sword include Benjamin F. Johnson, *My Life's Review*, ed. Lyndon W. Cook and Kevin B. Harker (Provo, UT: Grandin Book, 1997), 85; Mary Elizabeth Rollins Lightner, "Statement," February 8, 1902, L. Tom Perry Special Collections, Brigham Young University (hereafter cited as Perry Special Collections); Lightner, "Remarks by Sister Mary E. Lightener who was sealed to Joseph Smith in 1842," April 14, 1905, Perry Special Collections; and Lightner to Emmeline B. Wells, summer 1905, Perry Special Collections.
11. The word "Celestial" has been inserted in purple pencil between "God's" and "only."

16

Utah Penitentiary.
Aug 5ᵗʰ 1886.

Sister Marinda Goff:

In private talk one evening with
Our Seer and Prophet Joseph Smith,
Before he shared a martyr's fate,
To me in solemn words did state;
To him an angel did appear
Saying thus, in language clear,
"I hereby come for thee to warn
(While in his hand a sword was drawn—)
To take thee wives— this law obey
Or God in anger will thee slay."
'Twas eighteen hundred forty three.
This sacred law was shown to me
Which gives to man his loving wives
God's only Celestial path to endless lives.

Lorenzo Snow.

17

Utah Penitentiary
Aug 6th 1856

My Dear Le Roie:

Long time ago there came to me
A letter nice — direct from thee:
And though I answer now so late,
It gave me pleasure very great.

    Thy Mother be thou sure to mind,
    To sisters likewise very kind;
    To one and all you also should
    Gentlemanly be — Kind and good.

May God thee bless, my Dear Le Roie
And make thee wise — a noble boy,
So when thou doth become a man
Thy name be famous through the land.

    Affectionately
      Your Father
      Lorenzo Snow.

[17]
Utah Penitentiary
Aug 6th 1886

My Dear Le Roie:
    Long time ago there came to me
    A letter nice—direct from thee:
    And though I answer now so late,
    It gave me pleasure very great.
        Thy Mother be thou sure to mind,
        To sister likewise very kind;
        To one and all you also should
        Gentlemanly be—kind and good.
    May God thee bless, my Dear Le Roie
    And make thee wise—a noble boy,
    So when thou doth become a man
    Thy name be famous through the land.
                Affectionately
                  Your Father
                  Lorenzo Snow.

[18]

Utah Penitentiary
Aug 6th 1886

My Dear Minnie May:
    Sweet little One, my gentle May,
    To thee some words I wish to say:
    Spare no pains to please thy Mother,
    Kindness also show thy brother.
        Our Loren watch with strictest care
        Lest in his path there be some snare
        Which if it's seen, quick give alarm
        Lest pale he's laid in death's cold arms.[12]
    May angels guard my Minnie May,
    Thy father pray's each night and day,
    And make her very good and wise
    Because therein her glory lies.
                            Affectionately
                            Your Father
                            Lorenzo Snow.

---

12. The word "on" has been inserted in purple pencil after "in," and the "s" in "arms" has been struck out in purple pencil.

[19]
Utah Penitentiary
Aug 22nd 1886

Miss Isabel Ball:

Now swiftly wings the happy day—
Thy bitter tears all wipe away—
To-morrow week these sombre walls
Deliver up thy Father, Ball.
In all thy ways his counsel seek,
Good do to all—be gentle, meek,
In all life's scenes be true and bold
Have Spirit guide and conscience hold
Sway triumphant;—these do, Miss Ball,
So when from Earth above you're called
The Queenly crown for which[13] you've striv'n
To you, Dear Friend, will sure be giv'n.

Lorenzo Snow.

---

13. The last three letters of "which" are in gray pencil in another hand.

[20]

The Mother's Altered Prayer
By Helen E. Whitman.

The suffering infant slept;
The faithful mother kept
Her ceaseless vigil by the couch of pain,
And o'er its form so fair
She breathed an anxious prayer:
"Lord, bring my loved one back to health again".

Standing beside the bed,
"Oh, hush"! the father said,
"Such bitter grieving is not good for thee;
Canst thou not feel to say,
And in thy spirit pray
'Thy will be done', whate'er the end may be?"
Sobbing, she cried, "Ah, no!
I love my darling so,
I cannot, cannot ever give him up!
Thou, who the Cross did bear,
A thorny crown I wear,
Oh, from my lips remove this bitter cup!"

20

"The Mother's Altered Prayer.
By Helen E. Whitman.

The suffering infant slept;
The faithful mother kept
Her ceaseless vigil by the couch of pain,
And o'er its form so fair
She breathed an anxious prayer:
"Lord, bring my loved one back to health again".

Standing beside the bed,
"Oh, hush!" the father said,
"Such bitter grieving is not good for thee;
Canst thou not feel to say,
And in thy spirit pray
'Thy will be done', whate'er the end may be?"

Sobbing, she cried, "Ah, no!
I love my darling so,
I cannot, cannot ever give him up!
Thou, who the Cross did bear,
A thorny crown I wear,
Oh, from my lips remove this bitter cup!"

21

While thus she prayed and wept,
A troubled slumber crept
Over her weary spirit for a time;
Yet even in her dreams
To see her child she seems,
And follows him from youth manhood's prime.

And, oh! her noble boy
That once with hope and joy
And pride, had caused her loving heart to swell,
She sees temptation win,
Lead on in ways of sin,
And bring at last into a felon's cell.

They lead him forth to die,
Oh! hear that mournful cry:
"To him, O Lord, pity and pardon send!"
But a stern voice says "Nay,
Thou for his life didst pray;
Behold of thy rebellious wish the end."

She 'woke; but while she slept
A wondrous change had swept—
And borne him in the Savior's arms to dwell,
(over)

[21]

While thus she prayed and wept,
A troubled slumber crept
Over her weary spirit for a time;
Yet even in her dreams
To see her child she seems,
And follows him from youth [to] manhood's prime.
And, oh! her noble boy
That once with hope and joy
And pride, had caused her loving heart to swell,
She sees temptation win,
Lead on in ways of sin,
And bring at last unto a felon's cell.

They lead him forth to die,
Oh! hear that mournful cry:
"To him, O Lord, pity and pardon send!"
But a stern voice says "Nay,
Thou for his life didst pray;
Behold of thy rebellious wish the end."

She 'woke; but while she slept
A wondrous change had swept—
And borne him in the Savior's arms to dwell,

(over)

27

[22]
'Twas then her heart did say—
"Lord I did blindly pray;
My heavenly Father, Thou hast ordered well."

[23]
Utah Penitentiary
Aug 23—1886[14]

At 3.55 p.m. Marshal Dyer accompanied by Capt Greenman walked around the wall to the North east corner. He had Sprague (the Guard) call the men to that corner of the yard when he said.

Gentlemen:

You have all doubtless heard that five prisoners have escaped today. I have been disposed to be very lenient in the past but I find that I will have to enforce more strict discipline among you prisoners. I have not been in office long, but I am continually hearing of conspiracies and jobs being put up by men in the pit—more probably than you are aware of. I understand there is a talk of holding up one of the guards in the pit. I told the guards they would have to take their chances with the men; but I wish to warn you all, that if such a thing should occur, I will kill every man in the yard who does not prevent it. This may seem harsh, but I will do it. There are some good men in this yard and I hope you will all heed this warning. There is work to be done here and outside and I expect to work you. I am disposed to treat

---

14. This heading is in gray pencil but is apparently in the same hand as the text.

[24]
you well if you behave yourselves, but I will have to enforce stricter measures unless this thing is stopped. That is all gentlemen.

The prisoners scattered out in various directions, but before they had all passed out of hearing he stopped while walking westward on the North wall and said.

Gentlemen: I forgot to mention that there has been a fire started three or four times in the Bunk houses and I have instructed the Warden not to unlock the door if such a thing ever occurs again. That is all gentlemen.

[25]
Utah Penitentiary
Sept 1st 1886

Mrs Melissa Borlase:
> With faith in God in patience wait;
> Thy troubles soon will all be oer
> And thou wilt reign in Queenly state
> In realms above through countless years:—
> In youthful beauty constant grow;
> Then pain, nor death, nor flowing tears
> No longer shalt thou ever know;
> But countless years will mark thy fame
> And mighty growth of thy domain.

Lorenzo Snow.

[26]

Utah Penitentiary
Sept. 6, 1886

Bishop W. M. Bromley:

Our God who dwells in realms of light,
In flesh was veiled in sombre night,
Of woman born and there disrobed
Of all he knew in times of old.[15]
When years had flown in childhood scenes,[16]
His mighty past began to gleam,
More brightly grow 'till clearly shown
Once he was God and all things own'd.
So we there dwelt in shining climes
In honor bright, but now in time
These facts revealed—and wonder'us 'tis—
And perfect shown as man now is
Our God once was, as he's now seen
Man may be, 'cause true he's been[17]
In spirit-land there born of God—
A soul just like Christ, Jesus, Lord.
This holy path was also trod
By righteous men that now are Gods
As Abram, Isaac, Jacob too
First babes, then men, thence Gods they grew.

---

15. The word "what" is written in purple pencil above "all."
16. The word "rolld" is written in purple pencil above "had," and "from" is written in purple pencil above "flown in."
17. That God had once been a man and that man could become like God was a favorite theme of Snow's, which he expressed most concisely in his famous couplet, "As man now is, God once was: / As God now is, man may be." This doctrine had been revealed to him in the spring of 1840 while he was listening to H. G. Sherwood explain the parable of the husbandman and laborers; see Eliza R. Snow, *Biography and Family Record of Lorenzo Snow* (Salt Lake City: Deseret News, 1884), 46–47. Joseph Smith publicly taught the doctrine in his famous "King Follett Discourse" in 1844. For additional statements by Snow on this theme, see *The Teachings of Lorenzo Snow*, ed. Clyde Williams (Salt Lake City: Bookcraft, 1996), 1–9.

26

Utah Penitentiary
Sept. 6. 1886

Bishop W. M. Bromley:
Our God who dwells in realms of light,
In flesh was veiled in sombre night,
Of woman born and there disrobed
Of all he knew in times of old .
When years had flown in childhood scenes;
His mighty past began to gleam,
More brightly grow 'till clearly shown
Once he was God and all things own'd.
So we there dwell in shining climes
In honor bright, but now in time
These facts revealed — and wondering 'tis —
And perfect shown as man now is
Our God once was, as he's now seen
Man may be, 'cause true he's been
In spirit-land there born of God —
A soul just like Christ, Jesus, Lord,
This holy path was also trod
By righteous men that now are Gods
As Abram, Isaac, Jacob too
First babes, then men, thence Gods they grew.

27

Dear William, friend, this lofty hope
Will light thy way — yield power to cope
With trials fierce, bear safe thee on
O'er path o'er which the Gods have gone.
                              Lorenzo Snow

[27]

Dear William, friend, this lofty hope
Will light thy way—yield power to cope
With trials fierce, bear safe thee on
O'er path o'er which the Gods have gone.

Lorenzo Snow

[28]

Brigham City
Sept. 6, 1886.

Hon. Lorenzo Snow,
        Utah Penitentiary
My dear father:
O! Father dear, thy counsel wise
Which point to Him beyond the skies,
Thy daughter here, on earth below,
To thee, to man, to God will show
        She'll try to follow.

——————— " ———————

For well she knows if she but heed—
And, Father dear, how great's her need;
For wayward is the heart and wild
Of her who's proud to be thy child—
        She'll exalted be.

——————— " ———————

Yes, wayward is this heart of mine—
How great's the contrast unto thine—
But when in converse sweet with thee
This heart is calmed, this mind is free
        From temptation's trammels.

——————— " ———————

I then can smile at tempter's wile,
Marvel that he could e'er beguile.
I then can see with peaceful eye
that envyings, strife, all deep doth lie
      Afar below me.

———————— " ————————

My soul no longer strives within—
No warfare there: thou has banished sin;
But soars with thine in realms of love
To seek that home beyond, above
      This earth of ours.

———————— " ————————

Life then is sweet and worth the while
To live—within me no thought of guile;
No other aim, then my only ambition
To toil, to work, to gain salvation
      As taught by thee.

———————— " ————————

When e'er this influence's held,
The proud spirit within me's quelled;
A passionate longing fills my breast
To pierce the veil and view the rest
      That waits us there.

———————— " ————————

[30]
Death then is but a simple change
To life eternal that's in the range
Of all—the path's so clear and bright
I fear not, for a monitor of light
    Doth point the way.
—————— " ——————

O! Father dear, then give to me
That strength which like some magic key
To open doors where truth and light
Doth flood my soul, and wisdom's h[e]ight
    Is plain before me.
—————— " ——————

And by that strength I'll seek to be,
With God's help, a pride to thee,
In thy crown, a jewel bright and fair,
Which thou as martyr, King, wilt wear
    In our Heavenly Home.

Your daughter
Lydia.

—————— " ——————

[31]
Utah Penitentiary
Sept. 21, 1886

Sister Snelsen:
Beyond the realms of ether blue
There dwelt thy Spirit just and true,
And winged its way from thence to Earth
In Brigham town to take its birth.

———————— " ————————

Before thou left those lovely climes
To dwell on Earth these stormy times,
Thy labor here did God thee show[18]
Its purpose, kind, didst then thou know?

———————— " ————————

No doubt fair friend, though wondr'us true,
Thy path was shown, it well thou knew,
Yet, after veiled in sombre night
The fact was blotted from thy sight.

———————— " ————————

From early dawn—through morn of life
Ere thou became a lovely wife,
Thy God watched o'er thee, kept thee pure
To do thy work—enjoy—endure.

———————— " ————————

18. The word "thee" has been rendered "then" by placing the letter "n" in purple pencil over the second "e."

[32]
Though oft thy <u>mind</u> can't tell thee why
<u>This</u> thou should'st do, and <u>that</u> aught try[19]
Thy <u>heart</u> t'will never guide thee wrong,
What's right to do t'will prompt thee strong.

———————— " ————————

With Spirit pure, and heart so true
No guile wherein there ever grew,
With thee God's spirit therefore rests
And on thy heart clear truths impress.

———————— " ————————

Thy husband dear now oft recalls
Thy burdens borne 'mid cares and toils
With cloudless brow and smiling face—
With spirits bright and charming grace.

———————— " ————————

And cheering words, and counsels wise,
Didst prompt his heart and mind to rise
With added force to struggle through
His thorny path, inspired anew.

———————— " ————————

And truly feels thou well hast done
Thus far thy work for which thou'st come,
And still will do, with fervent love,
Thy offer made in realms above.

Lorenzo Snow.

———————————

19. A comma has been inserted in purple pencil after "try."

[33]
Utah Penitentiary
Sept. 25, 1886

<u>Dear Lydia:</u>
Well pleased I am as thus I see
Poetic fire light up in thee;
Awake thy muse and tune the lyre,
Discoursing thoughts I love—admire.

——————— " ———————

This well we know, and well you should
To thee hath God been wondr'us good
In giving thus this lofty mind,
With talents too of rarest kind.

——————— " ———————

Thy noble mind of gifts so grand
Must thoughts employ, and ready stand
To work for all with love supreme,
'Cause all have sprung from Eloheim.

——————— " ———————

When'er thou write, or hold converse—
As oft thou doth, and very terse—
Thy motive keep right well defined
'Tis naught but love that prompts thy mind.

——————— " ———————

[34]
Ah, more than once I've watched thee there
Amid thy noble sisters fair,
When, then thou spake with power, and taught
As God inspired each blazing thought.

———————— " ————————

With love, with zeal, and heart withal
Must ready do what God doth call—
To teach, instruct in Zion's cause—
Discourse, propound God's holy laws.[20]

———————— " ————————

If waters flow—if sun doth shine
Then God doth thee this work assign,
Will give thee light and power devine,
And fire thy heart—inspire thy mind.

———————— " ————————

And may thy fame through gifts so grand
Be herald o'er fair Zion's land;
High thought awake—vast names enroll
On high ambition's lofty scroll.

———————— " ————————

To father, husband, mother too
This honor high must flow from you,
And sweetest joy you'll <thus>[21] impart
As holy incense to our heart.
    Affectionately, your father, Lorenzo Snow.

---

20. The "s" in "laws" has been struck out in purple pencil.
21. The word "thus" is in purple pencil, written over and obscuring another word. The word "thus" is also written in purple pencil to the side of "impart."

[35]
Utah Penitentiary
Sept. 29, 1886

Mrs. E. R. S. Smith:

O, Sister dear, could I define
And write them sweet in lovely rhyme
My thoughts of thee,—a Sister's <u>love</u>
As burns in heart of queens above:—
    One moment catch poetic fire
    Arouse the muse and tune the lyre
    O, then I'd sing, my Sister dear,
    Of what thou'st been—and picture clear
Thy love to me:—beside, thy fame
Now wafted o'er the stormy main
Thence spread almost to ev'ry clime
And talked in tongues of many kind.
    Will live and blaze on hist'ry's page
    Be read by child, and thoughtful sage
    Till world by fire God's wrath infold
    From east to west, from pole to pole.
E'n then, behold thy name 'twill shine
In record kept of works of thine
By holy scribes in yonder sphere
Where thou a Godess will appear.

[36]
Thy love to me 'mid all the scenes
Of early youth, and downward stream[22]
Along life's course to gray old age,[23]
There blaze in each historic page.
More precious still 'cause penciled deep[24]
Down in my heart—to mem'ry sweet,
Most pure, and glows—immortal, chaste,
O, never can it be effaced.
We've frequent held converse together
Of pleasant kind, delightsome ever;
On wings of thought our mind would stray
Aloft, beyond the Milky Way.
There seek with care the realms of thought
In quest of pearls, dared not be sought
By timid mind devoid of force
To trace life's path, and view its source.
May God thee bless, thy life prolong,
Improve thy health, thy faith make strong,
Delight thy heart when calling o'er
Thy works of love, thy written lore.

Affectionately your Brother
Lorenzo Snow.

22. A comma has been added in purple pencil after "stream."
23. The word "life's" has been struck out with purple pencil, and "its" has been inserted.
24. The word "'cause" has been struck out with purple pencil, and "now" has been inserted.

[37]
Utah Penitentiary
Octr. 1, 1886

<u>Mrs M. J. Snow:</u>

I herewith send my congratulations to Ephraim and Hattie Jensen in the following lines, which please copy and send them:

<u>Mrs. M. J. Snow:</u>

That stirring news direct from you
Of Eph', my friend, and Hattie too,
Inspire my Muse to rise and sing
Their little prince—their embro' King.

———————— " ————————

This fact no doubt will time unfold
That little chap's a spirit bold
To waft itself from lovely climes
To 'bide on Earth such stormy times.[25]

———————— " ————————

All hail! sweet boy like magic grow
Your purpose here try quick to know
And e'en in youth an Ajax be
To help our God make Zion free.

Respectfully
Lorenzo Snow

———————————

25. The word "these" has been written in purple pencil above the word "such."

45

[38]

Utah Penitentiary
Octr. 4, 1886

Elder Stanley Taylor:
Fierce, cruel hands have torn from thee
That sacred boon, sweet liberty
And forced thee here Earth's lowest hell
To dwell forlorn in murders' cell.
     But list O, list, to what is told
     That 'fore this Globe from chaos rolled
     What there occurred—forgotten now,[26]
     Yet still those facts we should allow.[27]
Aloft beyond high ether blue
There Spirits dwelt, and also you
Were there amid that mighty host
Of noble souls each true and just.
     Thy name there stood in letters bold
     In sacred Book of life enrolled,
     By reason this 'cause thou hadst hailed
     With joyful heart what God unvailed:—
This purpose grand, those Spirits raise
Like Gods to be—explained the way;
And hence arose this promise thine
To come to Earth this stormy time:—

---

26. A dash has been inserted in purple pencil following "now."
27. The period has been changed to a semicolon in purple pencil.

38

Utah Penitentiary
Octr. 4, 1886

+ Elder Stanley Taylor:

Fierce, cruel hands have torn from thee
That sacred boon, sweet liberty
And forced thee here, Earths lowest hell
To dwell forlorn in murders' cell.
 But list O, list, to what is told
 That 'fore this Globe from chaos rolled
 What there occurred — forgotten now—
 Yet still those facts we should allow;
Aloft beyond high ether blue,
There Spirits dwell, and also you
Were there amid that mighty host
Of noble souls each true and just.
 Thy name there stood in letters bold
 In sacred Book of life enrolled,
 By reason this cause thou hadst hailed
 With joyful heart what God unvailed :—
This purpose grand, those Spirits raise
Like Gods to be — explained the way;
And hence arose this promise thine
To come to Earth this stormy time:—

39

Fierce trials meet devoid of fear,
Thy Priesthood too, thy calling here
With heart and soul to magnify
In doing which thy glory lies.
When forced within these prison walls
Thy heart thereby t'would never pall
But show to man and Gods on high
Thy wives thou never wouldst deny.

Lorenzo Snow.

[39]

Fierce trials meet devoid of fear,
Thy Priesthood too, thy calling here
With heart and soul to magnify
In doing which thy glory lies.
When forced within these prison walls
Thy heart thereby t'would never pall
But show to man and Gods on high
Thy wives thou never would'st deny.

Lorenzo Snow.

---

[40]

Salt Lake City, Octr. 4, 1886

<u>Response.</u>

<u>Hon. Lorenzo Snow:</u>
Your precious letter, Brother Dear,
So kind—so loving, drew a tear
From eyes whence tears are loth to flow
Except for others' weal or woe.

——————— " ———————

The tall expressions drawn by thee,
Seem far to grand t'apply to me;
But I admit all—all is true,
As you portrayed my love for you.

——————— " ———————

Your upright course has ever spread
A halo on the path I tread:
Your firm, unswerving life, from youth,
To age, has been for God and truth.

——————— " ———————

From north to south—from east to west,
Your willing feet the sands have press'd—
O'er boist'rous seas and oceans wave
You've gone—for what? Men's souls to save.

——————— " ———————

[41]

In your life-record, there is not
One silent page, nor one foul blot:
Eternal Archives yet will tell
Your every page is written well.

———————— " ————————

Yes, those <u>excelsior</u> interviews
Refreshing as Mount Hermon's dews
Bade thought on lofty flights to soar
Beyond the reach of worldly lore.

———————— " ————————

Now, in accordance with the fate
Of ancient Saints, the prison grate—
The prison walls, and prison fare
Attest your faith and patience there.

———————— " ————————

Thus was our Savior's legacy—
He said, "<u>All those who follow me</u>
<u>Shall suffer persecution</u>": and
He now is proving who will stand.

———————— " ————————

Obedience and sacrifice
Secure to you th'immortal prize—
You'll share with Christ his glorious reign,
And to the Godhead you'll attain.

———————— " ————————

[42]
God grant us wisdom, grace and power
To bravely stand the trying hour,
Till Zion pure, redeem'd, and free,
Moves on in peaceful majesty.

Lovingly,
Your Sister,
E. R. Snow Smith

———————— " ————————

Addenda
We need not scale Parnasus' height
To seek the Muse for aid t'indite
Nor wander through th'Arcadian grove
In search of Juno or her Jove.

———————— " ————————

The Inspiration God imparts,
T'instruct our heads, and warm our hearts;
Far better light and warmth diffuses,
Than e'er obtain'd from Pagan muses.

E.R.S.S

[43]
Utah Penitentiary
Octr. 1, 1886

Elder Willard L. Snow:
We feel no tears to shed for thee
When thy fair visage first we see,
Spy thee through the grate awaiting
To pass within the iron grating.

It gives a key no mortal made
Yet has it pow'r to mortals aid
'Cause we, though mortals, clearly see
By it, high virtue dwells in thee.

It ope's to us—this magic key—
What's in thy heart—integrity:—
No virtue told, is more sublime
Than this that's shown as truly thine.[28]

Thy presence here to us implies
Thou'rt not of those that shameful fly
From righteous post and wives deny
And make themselves a standing lie.

---

28. The word "this" is underlined in purple pencil.

[44]
Thrice welcome here, dear Willard Snow,
Our hearts to'ard thee with fervor glow.
And proud to see thyself thus fir'd
With spirit bold—by Gods admir'd.

But feel no tears to shed for thee
When thy fair visage first we see
Spy thee through the grate awaiting
To pass within the iron grating.

Lorenzo Snow.

[45]
Utah Penitentiary
Octr. 16, 1886.

Judge W. J. Cox,

    Dear Bro:

Sweet smiling June of Eighty seven
Will mark thee sixty one and 'leven,
Though white thy hair with winter frost
Thy vigor, force 'pears little lost.

    Though wrinkles deepen on thy brow
    No signs of dotage therein show:
    Through strength of mind and inward grace
    Old age sits smiling o'er thy face.

Time with thee's been gen'rous, kind,
And none withal impaired thy mind;
Thy speech denotes no careless haste,
Thy words are chosen, just and chaste.

    Thy heart most pure we easy trace
    In heavenly smiles that light thy face.
    Thy kindly face exhibits grace,
    Good humor too—all go to chase

Our gloomy thoughts—make us better
Thereby show we're some thy debtor.
Our God accepts thy offering here
Thyself hath given without a tear;

[46]
<u>Thyself</u> a lamb, a dove as pure,
Like Christ, this suffering doth endure.
All hail! friend Cox, All hail, my brother,
T'will not be long we'll greet each other
In realms on high where joys abound
And then, as promised, Gods be crowned.

Lorenzo Snow.

[47]
American Fork, U. T.
Octr. 13, 1886

Dear William:
Some gift on this thy Natal day,
As kindly homage would I pay,
Some happy song of greeting raise,
Of thy dear life, in gentle praise;
Oh! till thy latest living hour
May God his blessings on thee shower.

Rosena Bromley.

Utah Penitentiary, Octr. 19th. 1886
The following verses were written in answer to the above, in behalf
of Bishop Wm M. Bromley, by his request:—   Rosena Bromley:
Thy gift of love safe winged its way
To crown with joy my Natal day,
Nor locks nor bars could stay the course
Of love's sweet persevering force.

Were thousand worlds their jewels thine,
And proffered thou to make them mine,
'Twere naught but dross compared with those
Sweet, tender lines of thy compose.

[48]
Designed by bright angelic skill,
Thou had'st a song my soul to thrill,
T'would be but dross beside thy <u>verse</u>
Expressing thought both clear and terse.

Each line breathes love, each word a wish
To crown my Natal day with bliss.
That priceless love, deep in thy heart,
This truth implies, doth clear impart,

Thou'rt one in me—thy peerless self,
As I'm in thee; As Jesus saith,
"I'm in the Father, He In Me":
"Be thou my friends, as thus We be";

"Let love prevail with one another,"
"And every one prefer his brother."
Thy lines show wedded firm in love
Thy heart with mine—decreed above.

Perhaps, My Dear, t'was love inspired
Thy soul—which God himself admired—
To come with me on Earth, to plant
Thy kingdom here; and God did grant

[49]

That o'er it thou majestic reign
A peerless queen:—It n'er should wane,
But far beyond high ether blue
Where saints are crowned, each as his due,
To that fair clime should wing its way
And wax and roll through endless day.

Lorenzo Snow.

[50]

To my revered Freind

———— ″ ————

Lorenzo Snow.

First seen beyond the untold depths of ether,
    Whose subtle waves wash every shore of space;
In some grand Sun of Father's wide dominions
    Perchance in one He calls, His dwelling place!

———————— ″ ————— ″ —————

There, 'mid those nobles who were destined later,
    To tabernacle as the sons of men;
In this the last—and greatest—dispensation,
    To bear salvations message, learn'd e'en then!

———————— ″ ————— ″ —————

Next, seen on earth upon that favoured island
    Which was the mission field for men of God,
Who left the Prophet on the "western borders",
    Crossed States—the Ocean, for "Old Englands" sod.[29]

———————— ″ ————— ″ —————

Thence to "Italia" famed, and "Swiss Cantons",
    To ope' their doors to glorious gospel lights;
And give true freedom, to those ancient peoples,
    Who long had battled for the cause of right![30]

———————— ″ ————— ″ —————

Next seen in Utah, 'mid the gathered converts,
    The God-made leader, and the trusted friend;

---

29. Snow arrived in England as a missionary in October 1840. He preached in Liverpool, Manchester, and Birmingham before being called to preside over the newly created London Conference in February 1841. Under his leadership, the struggling London Conference swelled to several hundred members, dozens of whom had emigrated to the United States by the time Snow left England for Nauvoo in January 1843. See Andrew H. Hedges and Jay G. Burrup, "Shaping the Stones: Lorenzo Snow's Letters to Priesthood Leaders of the London Conference, November 1842," *BYU Studies* 38, no. 4 (1999): 8–9.
30. Snow opened Italy to missionary work on June 25, 1850, when he and two companions landed in Genoa. Spurned by the Italian Catholics, Snow and his companions had their greatest success among the Protestant Waldensians (or Waldenses) of Italy's Piedmont region, who had had fled there for safety after being excommunicated from the Catholic church in AD 1184. Snow spent a few days in Switzerland in February

50

+ To my Revered Friend
"
Lorenzo Snow.

First seen beyond the untold depths of ether,
Whose subtle waves wash every shore of space;
In some grand Sun of Father's wide dominions
Perchance in one He calls, His dwelling place.
— " — —

There, 'mid those nobles who were destined later,
To tabernacle as the sons of men;
In this the last and greatest dispensation,
To bear salvation's message, learn'd e'en then!
— " — " —

Next, seen on earth upon that favoured island
Which was the mission field for men of God,
Who left the Prophet on the "western borders",
Crossed States – the Ocean, for "Old England's" sod.
— " — " —

Thence to "Italia" famed, and "Swiss Cantons",
To ope' their doors to glorious gospel light,
And give true freedom, to those ancient peoples
Who long had battled for the cause of right.
— " — " —

Next seen in Utah, 'mid the gathered converts,
The God-made leader, and the trusted friend;

1852 en route from England, where he had overseen the translation of the Book of
Mormon into Italian, to Italy. Snow left Italy for Utah in March 1852.

61

51

Urging that culture, which the man discloses,
When mental force, and spirit knowledge blend.
___ " ___ " ___

Seen as the legislator,—statesman, shall I say?
On sure foundations, building up by law:
That Commonwealth, of Liberty and Right,
Which nations have not, yet the Prophets saw!
___ " ___ " ___

Then as the founder of industrial method,
For selfsustained, united family,
Where self is dormant, and the pride of labor,
Blesses the helpless, makes the toiler free.
___ " ___ " ___

More, as the minister of heaven, preaching
Those Truths eternal, which redeems our race
In all God's Zion, wheresoe'er her children,
Can plant a city, or secure a place!
___ " ___ " ___

In widening circles, influential, trusted,
A solid life, till age its power betrays;
A family great, from lives of honored station
Attests fidelity in lengthened days!
___ " ___ " ___

[51]

Urging that culture, which the man discloses,
When mental force, and spirit knowledge blend.[31]

———— " ———— " ————

Seen as the legislator,- statesman, shall I say?
On pure foundations, building up by law;
That Commonwealth, of Liberty and Right,
Which nations have not, yet the Prophets saw![32]

———— " ———— " ————

Then as the founder of industrial method,
For selfsustained, united family,
Where self is dormant, and the pride of labor,

[page 51 continued below]

31. An avid scholar, Snow was an active promoter of culture and education in Utah. Among other less formal efforts to enhance early Utah's intellectual life, he served as a regent of the University of Deseret; helped organize a Dramatic Association and public school system in Brigham City; and founded a "Polysophic Society" in Salt Lake City, the forerunner to the Church's Young Men's and Young Women's Mutual Improvement Associations (Heidi S. Swinton, "Lorenzo Snow," in *The Presidents of the Church*, ed. Leonard J. Arrington [Salt Lake City: Deseret Book, 1986], 163–64).
32. Snow served in the territorial legislature from 1852 to 1882, when he was disenfranchised as a result of the Edmunds Act. He had served as president of the Legislative Council from 1872 to 1882.

51

Urging that culture, which the man discloses,
When mental force, and spirit knowledge blend.

———— " ———— " ————

Seen as the legislator,—statesman, shall I say?
On sure foundations, building up by law;
That Commonwealth, of Liberty and Right,
Which nations have not, yet the Prophets saw!

———— " ———— " ————

Then as the founder of industrial method,
For selfsustained, united family,
Where self is dormant, and the pride of labor,
Blesses the helpless, makes the toiler free!

———— " ———— " ————

More, as the minister of heaven, preaching
Those Truths eternal, which redeems our race
In all God's Zion, wheresoe'er her children,
Can plant a city, or secure a place!

———— " ———— " ————

In widening circles, influential, trusted,
A solid life, till age its power betrays;
A family great, from wives of honored station
Attests fidelity in lengthened days!

———— " ———— " ————

Blesses the helpless, makes the toiler free![33]

——————— " ——————— " ———————

More, as the minister of heaven, preaching
Those Truths eternal, which redeems our race,
In all God's Zion, wheresoe'er her children,
Can plant a city, or secure a place!

——————— " ——————— " ———————

In widening circles, influential, trusted,
A solid life, till age its power betrays;
A family great, from wives of honored station,
Attests fidelity in lengthened days!

——————— " ——————— " ———————

---

33. At the request of Brigham Young, Snow had moved to Box Elder (later renamed Brigham City) in 1854 to preside over the saints in the area. Ten years later he organized several local retail stores into the Brigham City Co-operative Association, which generated enough profit for stockholders to build a tannery and shoe factory a few years later. Incorporated into the Brigham City Mercantile and Manufacturing Company in 1870, these three enterprises had grown to forty by 1874, supplying virtually all of the goods and services residents needed in the area. Leonard J. Arrington, Feramorz Y. Fox, and Dean L. May, *Building the City of God: Community and Cooperation among the Mormons* (Urbana and Chicago: University of Illinois Press, 1992), 111–15. Encouraged by Brigham City's successes, Brigham Young in 1874 began establishing "United Orders" in communities throughout the territory.

[52]

Then, when a busy life should claim its resting,
  'Mid joys of home, and with his gathered sheaves,[34]
When all would say, a Godlike past entitles
  To all that honor which the soul perceives.

——————— " ——————— " ———————

Yet, not in such a well assured position
  Could enemies have triumph,—is he found,
But in a prison, for his lifelong fealty
  To Truth, and Revelations certain sound!

——————— " ——————— " ———————

Patient and passive, waiting law's delaying,
  And paying penalty imposed of hate;
Feeling, that Justice, far hath fled away
  From Utahs soil, whose fame he helped create.

——————— " ——————— " ———————

Where next? Ah where, my months are nearly done,[35]
  There shall leave him, mid a changing {throng}
But I my homage pay to steadfast honor
  And pray that God may yet his life prolong!

——————— " ——————— " ———————

For friends, and for his sister weary growing
  With weight of years, and duties of the day;
Whose name—a household word—will linger ever,
  And songs be sung, when we have passed away!

---

34. The word "sheaves" is placed above "gathered," as the author ran out of space for the last word on this line. Similarly, on the previous line the word "resting" is placed above "claim its."
35. The word "done" is placed above "nearly."

[53]

But yet, if this should fail, and no more greeting,
    We meet as workers in that cause we love,—
<u>There is a meeting</u>, for the faithful coming,
    Beyond the stars, a heaven of perfect love!

————— " ————— " —————

There, also ~~is a~~ welcome is, from brave ones, sainted,[36]
    From Prophets, Martyrs, sages, of the past;
There God will wipe all tears from eyes now weeping,
    And crown his nobles, from the first to last!

————— " ————— " —————

May I, a humble server, find a station,
    If but <in> those grand courts, to simply show;
I loved the servants of my God and Father,
    Counting among the few,—<u>Lorenzo Snow!</u>

————— " ————— " —————

                     Henry W. Naisbitt.

————— " ——— " —————

Utah Penitentiary,
    Nov 7th 1886.

————— " " —————

---

36. The word "sainted" is written above "brave ones."

67

[54]

Utah Penitentiary
Octr. 28, 1886

Miss Mary Alice Lambert:
Be just to all, be gen'rous, kind,
And parents' wishes keep in mind,
By counsel theirs, be ever led,
God's word regard—it's in thee bred.

In thy dear self, O let us find
A bright and ever stud'ous mind
By habit formed through mental drill,
The shining fruit of sternest will.

Thy Father here, from him could'st take
A lesson thou—high profit make.
From earliest morn, long into night
Behold him! Seen with spirit bright

In mental toil—all play disdains—
Which constant toil vast knowledge gains,
Will prove of service vastly great
When raised, through worth, to high estate.

[55]

May thorns but little strew thy path
Sufficient just, to show contrast
Between the bitter and the sweet;
With that except: thy ready feet

    Will lightly tread the path of life
    Through flowery fields of pleasures rife,
    And need not "sleep" should death ensue;
    O let this thought thy heart imbrue.

Lorenzo Snow.

[56]

Miss Maria Burrows:
Here, below, my name's imbedded;
Above; my location headed.
The first; when seen, my heart takes ease
In fondest hope, t'will not displease;
 Of last; 'tis shown thou hast no fear
 From fact, thou'st placed thine Album here.
 Though locked at night in murderers' cell
 That's thought to be earth's lowest hell;
Yet time here, still, with pleasure flies,
No groans we hear, no sobs, no sighs.
'Twas not that we'd the law defy,
'Twas 'cause we'd not our wives deny
 That here we're placed in vile duress,
 To spirit crush, and truth repress;
 Deny our God, repent what's done,
 And so most shamefully become
Servile, fawning, race of dastards;
Serve our offspring same as bastards;
Our sweetest babes, our lovely girls,
Our smiling child of silken curls,

[57]

Our noble sons of heav'nly birth;
Jewels! All! All! Of priceless worth.
Our hearts disdain that monstrous sin,
Such awful guilt shall fail to win.
    'Twas Great Jehovah, gave us wives,
    His pointed path to endless lives.
    Our heart His Spirit oft o'er flows,
    When sweetest love then burns and glows.[37]
When thoughts arise of blessings vast
By Him bestowed in seasons past
Our present state we don't deplore,
Nor <u>fear</u> to sacrifice yet more.

Lorenzo Snow.

---

37. The period is replaced with a semicolon in purple pencil.

[58]

Utah Penitentiary
Nov. 13. 1886.

Mrs. Lydia S. Clawson:
From world above to world below
Just five and twenty years ago,
Pure, true, and brave, thy spirit came,
In noble deeds, here to proclaim

That virtue, love, together still
Unite in one the heart to thrill;
And kingdom start in embryo
That would to mighty nations grow.

And prove thy worth in God's esteem
Thy kingdom thus to reign its queen:
Deep in thy heart was seated love
Of God inspired in climes above

Thy Rudger Clawson thus to bring
Establish him its lord and king.
Thou pioneer of sisters brave
In prison first thy lord to save;

[59]

He being first of noble men
With honor graced our gloomy "Pen".
It truly may be said of thee
Yet, <u>here</u>, <u>still</u> prisoned would'st thou be

Instead of him, our God-like broth'r
Had'st thou <u>thy</u> will, and took no oth'r.
Hail! Sister brave, most noble wife,
Devoid of fear mid hotest strife

To fiercely wrest from husband thine
Rights most precious, e'en rights divine.
That thou cam'st here, resolved and bold,
Long to remain, has oft been told;

Thy husband's love straight that forbid,
Quick ordered thee from prison led.
Such love supreme, such love divine
Will blaze in this grand deed of thine,

Long down through ages, number vast.
Among the first—of them not last—
Of sisters thine—heroic band—
Thy name in bold relief shall stand

[60]
To help adorn historic page
More bright than that of king or sage;
And here thy work when finished seen
In glory reign Celestial Queen.

Lorenzo Snow.

[61]
Utah Penitentiary
Nov. 15. 1886

Mrs <u>Catherine</u> <u>H.</u> <u>Groesbeck</u>:
While in rambling there around
I met thee first in Brigham town;
Where 'mong thy friends thou wisely stray'd
When sorely pressed by fiendish raid,

    I thought thee <u>then</u> a heroine
    Nor changed this thought e'en since that time:
    <u>Now</u>, here I find thy Nicholas
    'Bout which the Courts made mighty fuss;

His noble mien, and stately frame,
His well deserved far spreading fame
From mission past, far more this last,—
His mission here—in prison cast;

    Thus show to world, and Gods on high
    His loyal wives he'd not deny.
    Since him I've learned; in choice of mate
    I think thee wise, discernment great.

[62]
Since thou a wife, vast work hast wrought
In that a Prince to him hast brought,
Sweet Princess too, just now I'm told
Thy glo'rous work doth still unfold.

Thy kingdom thus grandly started
Shall never be by Satan blasted,
But on, and on to nations grow
And on and up from here below

To empire rise in realms above,
Thou o'er it reign its Queen of love;
And he whose love hast made thee wife
There reign its king through endless life.

Lorenzo Snow.

[63]
Utah Penitentiary
Decr. 4, 1886.

My Boudoir,
'Tis, no doubt, you well remember
My neat, cozy, sleeping chamber,
Yet our friends 'twill not displease
Somewhat to know—their hearts twill ease,

So thus their fears entire disarm—
How nice we're fixed by "Uncle Sam".
Though oft he fails to full comply
With all we wish, all wants supply;

Yet him we hold in high disdain,
The poor ingrate that would complain.
Two feet, if add two inches more
My Boudoir starts from building floor;

Just four feet wide, its length 'tis seven,
Though much preferred if eight by 'leven.
For floor; rough boards on scantling stayed,
Wire cot o'er this correctly laid;

[64]
Then comes my mat, of wool it's made,
Then cotton sheets o'er that displayed;
Then blankets too in some profusion
Arranged entire without confusion;

    Then pillows common come in play
    Them modest crown without display.
    In inches, height is thirty six,
    Through blundering thought too oft we mix

Heads with ceiling, this though needless,
Wholly caused through being heedless.
The boards o'er head with ticking lined,
The same long down the wall behind;

    This ticking shows black lines prolonged
    O'er length and breadth—'tis truth and song;
    Large, square, white spots those lines infold
    Make pattern 'pear quite loud and bold,

In light of morn we curious gaze
And wonder where its beauty lays;
Such thoughts though needless here to waste,
'Cause much we vary in our taste.

[65]

A damask curtain, somewhat used
By careless maid, or time abused,
Flows down in front, with flowers adorned,
Nice, pattern sweet, artistic formed.

Thick, heavy cloth our heads behind
Divide two beds, to four assigned;
Below, at foot, board wide and strong
Preserves our rights, none venture wrong.

When lying prone along our bed
And pillows soft uphold our head,
'Bout fifteen inches measured space
Divide this ceiling from our face.

A nice planed board along one end
My Books thereon they gently bend:
Some magazines, your Juvenile,[38]
There in high worth and beauty smile,

Thoughts vastly rich—in purpose grand—
T'instruct our youth throughout the land,
E'en riper age from thence could store
A vast amount of classic lore.

---

38. The *Juvenile Instructor* was the Church's semimonthly Sunday School magazine. Founded and originally edited by George Q. Cannon in January 1866, it remained in the Cannon family until 1901, when the Deseret Sunday School Union purchased it. Renamed the *Instructor* in 1929, it continued until 1970. See Arnold K. Garr, Donald Q. Cannon, and Richard O. Cowan, eds., *Encyclopedia of Latter-day Saint History* (Salt Lake City: Deseret Book, 2000), 595–96.

[66]
Devoid of much this pretty trimming
Few other rooms are quite so winning;
Our "Sam" finds room, straw, and ticking,
(Sorry chance for 'ficial picking)

    Two blankets each for every man
    All else 'twere useless to demand;
    These facts herein are thus disclosed
    To 'muse the young, inform the old.

                      Lorenzo Snow.

To Abram H. Cannon,
    Juvenile Instructor Office
        Salt Lake City.

[67]
Utah Penitentiary
Decr. 7, 1886

Brother H. P. Folsom:
Now I have some moments leisure,
Here I'll state in lines of measure
When first with you in prison meeting
I felt such joy in thee greeting.[39]

I saw quite clear this fact unfold
Wherein these bars did'st thee enfold,
Thy steadfast heart—its precious worth—
To honor God while here on earth.

And boldly tread this thorny way;
No sacrifice would thee dismay
Nor terrors in this course should fright
Thee into path to endless night.

But thou thy God would'st glorify,
His holy law should'st not deny,
In him would'st trust, him would'st obey,
And coming here those facts display.

Lorenzo Snow.

---

39. The word "much" is written above "such" in another hand.

[68]

Utah Penitentiary
Decr. 25, 1886.

Miss Lizzie Cutler:
We're pleased to see your album here
Wherein you wish our name appear,
And pleased you're not as we now are
The subject of the Warden's care.

Lorenzo Snow.

——————— ″ ———————

Miss Delilia Gardner:
Your anxious wish to gratify,
My autograph you'll find below,
And furthermore, Dear friend thereby
My kind regards—Lorenzo Snow.

——————— ″ ———————

Miss Needham:
On thee, Dear friend, may God bestow
His blessings choice—Lorenzo Snow.

——————— ″ ———————

Miss Ann Turner:
On thee, Dear friend, may God bestow
His blessings choice—Lorenzo Snow

——————— ″ ———————

[69]
Utah Penitentiary
Jany. 4, 1887

Elder Jens Hansen:
Six weary months in Utah prison
At last, behold! your bonds are riven
Your cheerful voice no more we hear
Nor in your "Cell" you there appear.

Now freedom's flag it proudly waves
O'er you, the just, the true and brave:
While some would shun this sacrifice,
Withhold the cost that wins the prize;

Not so with thee, but joined the throng
Of willing martyrs—thus thy song—
As told by John, that none could sing
Save those to God would honor bring:—
Which thou could'st learn and worthy be,
There, on that brilliant, glassy sea
In shining robes, in glory stand
'Mong martyred saints with Christ, the Lamb.[40]

Lorenzo Snow.

---

40. See Revelation 4:4–11.

[70]

Utah Penitentiary
Jany 5. 1887.

Miss Rhoda Groesbeck:
Though pleased to see your Album here,
Would be more pleased could you appear,
Though not in bonds as we now are
The subject of the Warden's care;

——————— " ———————

But your nice organ with you bring,
Thereon perform—converse, or sing;
But here, the truth I freely own
Such favor choice cannot be shown.

——————— " ———————

Will, therefore, now my wish express
That Thee, our God will richly bless,
Thy trials make all easy, light,
And strew thy path with roses bright.

Lorenzo Snow.

[71]

December 25, 1886.

"Lorenzo Snow Esq.
 Compliments of
 Minna Cannon."

The above was accompanied by a beautifully ornamented raisin cake.

"Christmas Greetings
 To Dear Papa
"Dearest Pa, with joy we greet you
On, now this happy Christmas morn,
Yet because, that we must miss you,
These blessings much thereby are shorn.[41]

"

"While you've suffered, we acknowledge
Our present loss is future gain:
And we hope now soon to see you,
And have you with us once again.
                                Le Roie, Mable & Lore"

The above was accompanied by a nice Silk Handkerchief, the S.L. Temple woven on each corner.

---

41. Portions of "thereby are shorn" are written over with a dark blue ink, possibly in another hand.

[72]

"December 25, 1886"

"A Happy New Year
   With the Compliments of
      Lydia S. Clawson."

The above was accompanied by a pair of beautiful worsted wristlets

[73]

Copy⁴²

Utah Penitentiary
Jany. 9. 1887.

Hon. Jno. T. n,
Washington, D.C.

Dear Brother:

Herewith, you will find a letter addressed to President Cleavland. Realizing that very many of the communications addressed to the President and sent by mail never reach him, but find their way into the waste basket, I decided to enclose this one to you. As it is an <u>important</u> letter, you will greatly oblige me by seeing that it is placed in his hands.

My health, as also that of the brethern, is at present very good. We are looking forward, of course, with much interest to the decision of the Supreme Court relative to segregation.⁴³

Hoping that you are meeting with good success in your labors, I remain

Your bro. + c.,

Lorenzo Snow.

The following is a copy of the letter above referred to:

---

42. The word "Copy" is written on an angle at the top of the page.

43. Snow, having already served his first six months' prison sentence, is referring here to his appeal to the United States Supreme Court that his second and third convictions for unlawful cohabitation were illegal, as cohabitation was a single continuous offense that could not be divided, or "segregated," into discrete offenses on any other than an arbitrary basis. The court heard the case on January 21, 1887, and decided in his favor on February 7, 1887. See Firmage and Mangrum, *Zion in the Courts*, 182, and Ken Driggs, "Lorenzo Snow's Appellate Court Victory," *Utah Historical Quarterly* 58, no. 1 (Winter 1990): 81–93.

[74]

Utah Penitentiary
Jany 9, 188[7].

To the Hon. Grover Cleavland,
    President of the United States,[44]

Sir:

I herewith respectfully submit for your consideration the following facts: I am twenty nine years of age. In November 1884, I was convicted of Polygamy and Unlawful Cohabitation, and sentenced by Chas. S. Zane to four years imprisonment, and to pay a fine of $800.⁰⁰. I have now served out two years and two months of this sentence. That to which I particularly desire to direct your attention is this: When I entered the prison, <u>fourteen</u> of its inmates were undergoing punishment for <u>murder</u>, five having been sentenced for life, and the remainder, with two exceptions, for a long term of years.

Of this number, <u>nine</u> have gone out on a full and free pardon, two have been released, and three only remain, one of whom being a life man.

The immediate outgrowth of my alleged

---

44. This salutation is underlined in red ink.

74

Utah Penitentiary
Jany 9. 1886.

To the Hon. Grover Cleavland,
          President of the United States,
Sir:
          I herewith respectfully submit for your
consideration the following facts: I am twenty
nine years of age. In November 1884, I was con-
-victed of Polygamy and Unlawful Cohabitation, and sentenced by Chas. S. Zane to four years
imprisonment, and to pay a fine of $800.— I have
now served out two years and two months of
this sentence. That to which I particularly
desire to direct your attention is this: When
I entered the prison, fourteen of its inmates
were undergoing punishment for murder, five
having been sentenced for life, and the remainder,
with two exceptions, for a long term of years.
          Of this number, nine have gone out on a
full and free pardon, two have been released,
and three only remain, one of whom being a
life man.
          The immediate outgrowth of my alleged

WITHIN THESE PRISON WALLS

75

crime is life, of their crime, death.

A proposition has been made to me, as also to others of my faith, that if I would promise to obey the law in the future, as construed by the courts, I should receive a pardon; while, on the other hand, no such requirement whatever was made of the parties mentioned. Why, then, I respectfully ask, should a promise be required of me and not of them? And what, Mr President, will justify a leniency extended to one class of criminals— those who are guilty of murder, as against another class— those who are guilty of a misdemeanor only?

Respectfully,

Rudger Clawson.

[75]
crime is <u>life</u>, of their crime, <u>death</u>.

A proposition has been made to me, as also to others of my faith, that if I would promise to obey the law in the future, <u>as construed by the courts</u>, I should receive a pardon; while, on the other hand, no such requirement whatever was made of the parties mentioned. Why, then, I respectfully ask, should a promise be required of me and not of them? And what, Mr President, will justify a leniency extended to one class of criminals—those who are guilty of murder, as against another class—those who are guilty of a misdemeanor only?

Respectfully,
Rudger Clawson.[45]

45. For more on Clawson and his prison experience, see Rudger Clawson, *Prisoner for Polygamy: The Memoirs and Letters of Rudger Clawson at the Utah Territorial Penitentiary, 1884–87*, ed. Stan Larson (Urbana and Chicago: University of Illinois Press, 1993).

[76]

Names of brethern confined in the Utah
Penitentiary for Polygamy and Unlawful Co-habitation[46]

No	Age	Name	Residence	Term	Fine	Date of Imp[t].	By whom sentenced
1	24	Rudger Clawson	Salt Lake City	P. C.[47] 4 yrs	$800.⁰⁰	Nov. 3, 84	Zane
2	58	J. H. Evans	do	P 3½ "	500.	" 8, 84	"
3	48	P. P. Pratt	do	6 mos	300.	May 2. 85	"
4	51	A. M Cannon	do	6 "	300.	" 9 "	"
5		A. M Musser	do	6 "	300.	" 9 "	"
6	41	Jas. E. Watson	do	6 "	300	" 9 "	"
7	59	W^m. Fotheringham	Beaver	3 "	300	" 18 "	Boreman
8	63	F.A. Brown	Ogden	6 "	300.	July 11 "	Powers
9	45	Moroni Brown	do	6 "	300.	" 11 "	"
10	48	Job Pingree	do	6 "	300+c	" 15 "	"
11	59	H. B. Clawson	Salt Lake City	6 "	300+c	Sept. 29 "	Zane
12	55	John Lang	Beaver	3 "	300	" 29 "	Boreman
13	65	Edwd. Brain	Salt Lake City	6 "	300.+c	Oct 2 "	Zane
14	51	Chas. Seal	do	6 "	300+c.	" 5 "	"
15	44	D. E. Davis	Tooele	6 "	300.+c	" 5 "	"
16	59	Isaac Groo	Salt Lake City	6 "	300. c	" 5 "	"
17	56	Alfred Best	do	6 "	300. c	" 5 "	"
18	49	A.W. Cooley	do	6 "	300. c	" 5 "	"
19	28	C. L. White	do	6 "	300 c	" 6 "	"
20	33	Jno. Connelly	do	6 "	300. c	" 6 "	"
21	43	W. A. Rossiter	do	6 "	300. c	" 10 "	"
		Total months & Fine:—		**198**	**$ 7000.**		

---

46. The following table is drawn up in the text of the letterbook in pink ink, but the entries are made in dark ink.
47. "Prisoner in custody."

76 Names of brethern confined in the Utah Penitentiary for Polygamy and Unlawful Cohabitation

No	Age	Name	Residence	Term	Fine	Date of Impt	By whom Sentenc'd
1	24	Rudger Clawson	Salt Lake City	4 yrs	800.=	Nov. 3. 84	Zane
2	58	J. H. Evans	do.	3½	500.	" 8. 84	"
3	48	P. P. Pratt	do	6 mos	300.	May 2. 85	"
4	51	A. M. Cannon	do	6 "	300.	" 9 "	"
5		A. M. Musser	do	6 "	300.	" 9 "	"
6	41	Jas. E. Watson	do.	6 "	300	" 9 "	"
7	59	Wm. Fotheringham	Beaver	3 "	300	" 18 "	Boreman
8	63	F. A. Brown	Ogden	6 "	300	July 11	Powers
9	45	Moroni Brown	, do	6 "	300.	" 11.	"
10	45	Job Pingree	do	6 "	300 +c	" 15.	"
11	59	H. J. Clawson	Salt Lake City	6 "	300 +c	Sept 29.	Zane
12	55	John Lang	Beaver	3 "	300	" 29.	Boreman
13	65	Edwd. Brain	Salt Lake City	6 "	300 +c	Oct 2	Zane
14	51	Chas. Seal	do	6 "	300 +c	" 5 "	"
15	44	J. E. Davis	Tooele	6 "	300 +c	" 5 "	"
16	59	Isaac Groo	Salt Lake City	6 "	300. c	" 6 "	"
17	56	Alfred Best	do	6 "	300. c	" 5 "	"
18	49	A. W. Cooley	do	6 "	300 c	" 5 "	"
19	28	C. L. White	do	6 "	300 c	" 6 "	"
20	33	Jno. Connelly	do	6 "	300. c	" 6 "	"
21	43	W. A. Rossiter	do	6 "	300. c	" 10 "	"
		Total months & Fine :-		198	7000.		

77

No.	Age	Name	Residence	Term	Fine	Date of Imph.	By whom Sentenced
22	54	Geo. Romney	Salt Lake City	6 mos	300. c	Oct 10	Zane
23	36	Emil O. Olsen	do	6 .	300 c	. 13 .	.
24	46	Jno. Nicholson	do	6 .	300. c	. 13 .	.
25	49	Andrew Smith	do	6 .	300 c	. 13 .	.
26	53	Aurelius Miner	do	6 .	300. c	. 14 .	.
27	50	W= D. Newsom	do	3½ yrs	300. c	. 14 .	.
28	50	Robt. H. Swain	do	6 mos	300. c	Nov 2 .	.
29	41	Fredk. H. Hansen	West Jordan	6 .	300 c	. 5 .	.
30	44	Thos Porcher	Salt Lake City	6 .	300 c	. 21 .	.
31	35	J. W. Keddington	do	6 .	300. c	. 21 .	.
32	68	Henry Gale	Beaver	6 .	300. c	Dec 14	Boreman
33	50	Culbert King	Marion	6 .	300 c	. 25 .	.
34	51	J. E. Twitchel	Indian Creek	6 .	300 c	. 25 .	.
35	69	D. M. Stewart	Ogden	6 .	300 c	Jan 4	Powers
36	46	Jas. H. Nelson	do	6 .	300 c	. 16 .	.
37	44	W. W. Willey	Bountiful	5 .	200 c	Feb. 10 .	Zane
38	51	Jno. Penman	do	2 yrs	25 c	. 10 .	.
39	42	Robt Morris +	Salt Lake City	6 mos	150 c	. 16 .	.
40	46	Thos. Burmingham	Bountiful	6 .	300 c	. 14 .	.
41	44	Jno Powen	Tooele	6 .	300 c	. 14 .	.
42	68	Wm G. Saunders	Ogden	12 .	25. c	. 18 .	Powers
		Total months + Fines:—		344	12.500		

[77]

No.	Age	Name	Residence	Term	Fine	Date of Impt.	By whom sentenced
22	54	Geo. Romney	Salt Lake City	198 6 mos	7000. 300. c	Oct.10. 85	Zane
23	36	Emil O. Olsen	do	6 "	300 c	" 13. "	"
24	46	Jno. Nicholson	do	6 "	300. c	" 13 "	"
25	49	Andrew Smith	do	6 "	300 c	" 13 "	"
26	53	Aurelius Miner	do	6 "	300. c	" 17 "	"
27	50	Wᵐ D. Newsom	do	P. 3½ yrs.	300. c	" 17 "	"
28	50	Robt. H. Swain	do	6 mos.	300. c	Nov.2 "	"
29	41	Fredᵏ. H. Hansen	West Jordan	6 "	300. c	" 5 "	"
30	47	Thos Porcher	Salt Lake City	6 "	300. c	" 21 "	"
31	35	J. W. Keddington	do	6 "	300. c	" 21 "	"
32	68	Henry Gale	Beaver	6 "	300. c	Dec.17 "	Boreman
33	50	Culbert King	Marion	6 "	300 c	" 25 "	"
34	51	J. E. Twitchel	Indian Creek	6 "	300 c.	" 25 "	"
35	59	D. M. Stewart	Ogden	6 "	300. c	Jan. 4. 86	Powers
36	46	Jas. H. Nelson	do	6 "	300 c	" 16 "	"
37	44	W. W. Willey	Bountiful	5 "	200 c	Feb.10 "	Zane
38	51	Jno. Penman	do	P. 2 yrs.	25 c	" 10 "	"
39	42	Robt. Morris	Salt Lake City	6 mos.	150 c	" 16 "	"
40	46	Thos.Burmingham	Bountiful	6 "	300 c	" 17 "	"
41	44	Jno. Bowen	Tooele	6 "	300 c	" 17 "	"
42	68	Wᵐ. G. Saunders	Ogden	12 "	25. c	" 18 "	Powers
		Total months & Fine:—		377	$ 12.500.		

[78]

No	Age	Name	Residence	Term	Fine	Date of Impt.	By whom sentenced
43	47	S. H. Smith	Salt Lake City	377 6 mos.	12.500 300 c	Feb. 20. 86	Zane
44	60	H. Dinwoodey	do	6 "	300 c	" 23 "	"
45	64	Jos. McMurrin	do	6 "	300 c	" " "	"
46	49	Amos. Maycock	Ogden	11 "	100. c	" 24 "	Powers
47	49	W^m. H. Lee	Tooele	6 "	300. c	" 26 "	Zane
48	54	Hugh S Gowans	Tooele	6 "	300 c	" 26 "	"
49	38	H. J. Foulger	Salt Lake City	6 "	300 c	" 26 "	"
50	37	H. H. Tracy	Ogden	12 "	no	" 26 "	Powers
51	29	C. W. Greenwell	do	6 "	300. c	" 26 "	"
52	57	J. P Ball	Salt Lake City	6 "	300 c	" 27 "	Zane
53	52	Jno Y. Smith	do	6 "	300. c	" 27 "	"
54	61	Thos. C. Jones	do	6 "	300. c	" 27 "	"
55	50	Jas. Moyle	do	6 "	300 c	Mch 1 "	"
56	36	S. F. Ball	do	6 "	300 c	" 1 "	"
57	59	Jas. O. Poulsen	West Jordan	6 "	300 c	" 1 "	"
58	56	Geo. H. Taylor	Salt Lake City	6 "	300 c	" 1 "	"
59	50	O. F. Due	do	6 "	300 c	" 1 "	"
60	35	Hyrum Goff	West Jordan	6 "	300 c	" 3 "	"
61	44	W. J. Jenkins	do	6 "	300 c	" 3 "	"
62	48	Fred^k. A. Cooper	do	6 "	300 c	" 8 "	"
63	44	Jno. W. Snell	Salt Lake City	6 "	300 c	" 9 "	"
		Total months & Fine:—		**514**	**$ 18,300**		

No	Age	Name	Residence	Term	Fine	Date of Impt.	By whom sentenced
64	72	Lorenzo Snow	Brigham City	514 18 mos.	18300 900. c	Mch 12. 86	Powers
65	27	Abram Cannon	Salt Lake City	6 "	300 c	" 17 "	Zane
66	58	Robt. McKendrick	Tooele	6 "	300. c	" 18 "	"
67	40	L. D. Watson	Parowan	6 "	300 c	" 27 "	Boreman
68	37	L. J. Bates	Monroe	3 "	100. c	Apl.14 "	Powers
69	46	Wm Grant	Am. Fork	4 "	——	" 14 "	"
70	63	Jno Bergen	Salt Lake City	2 yrs	1200.c	" 26 "	Zane
71	48	Stanley Taylor	do	6 mos	300. c	May 10 "	"
72	44	Andrew Jensen	Mill Creek	6 "	300 c	" 10 "	"
73	53	G. B. Bailey	do	6 "	300 c	" 10 "	"
74	38	Geo C. Lambert	Salt Lake City	6 "	300 c	" 11 "	"
75	56	H. W. Naisbitt	do	6 "	300. c	" 11 "	"
76	59	Levi Minnerly	Wellsville	5 "	——	" 25 "	Powers
77	29	R. C. Smith	do	6 "	——	" 25 "	"
78	53	Ambrose Greenwell	Ogden	12 "	300 c	" 26 "	"
79	61	M. L Shepperd	Beaver	6 "	300 c	" 28 "	Boreman
80	44	W. G. Bickley	do	6 "	300 c	" 28 "	"
81	44	P. Wimmer	do	6 "	300 c	" 28 "	"
82	71	Wm. J. Cox	do	6 "	300 c	" " "	"
83	32	Geo. C. Wood	Bountiful	P. C 5 yrs 3 mos.	800 c	June 1 "	Powers
84	34	Royal B. Young	Salt Lake City	18 mos.	900 c	" 1 "	Zane
		Total months & fine:—		732	$ 26.100		

[80]

No	Age	Name	Residence	Term	Fine	Date of Impt.	By whom sentenced
85	36	Chas. Denney	Salt Lake City	732 6 mos.	26.100 300 c	June. 1. 86	Zane
86	47	L. H. Berg	do	6 "	300 c	" 1 86	"
87	49	Jens Hansen	Mill Creek	6 "	300 c	" 2 "	"
88	65	W^m. Stimpson	Ogden	8 "	300 c	" 5 "	Powers
89	54	W. H. Pidcock	do	13 "	——	" 30 "	"
90	44	N. H. Groesbeck	Springville	9 "	450 c	Aug 2 "	"
91	46	Wm M. Bromley	Am. Fork	10 "	300 c	" 3 "	"
92	72	Wm Felsted	Salt Lake City	P. 3^2 yrs	250 c	Sep. 14 "	Zane
93	56	Richd Warburton	Tooele	6 mos.	300 c	" 20 "	"
94	55	J. E. Lindberg	do	18 "	300 c	" 20 "	"
95	58	Wm W. Jeffs[48]	Salt Lake City	19 "	400 c	" 22 "	"
96	48	W. W. Galbraith	Kaysville	6 "	300 c	" 22 "	"
97	49	Jas. Dunn	Tooele	12 "	300 c	" 23 "	"
98	45	H. P. Folsom	Salt Lake City	6 "	300 c	" 25 "	"
99	55	Wm Robinson	Beaver	6 "	300 c	" 26 "	Boremen
100	64	Geo. Hales	do	6 "	300 c	" " "	"
101	59	Thos. Schofield	do	6 "	300 c	" " "	"
102	63	Jas. Farrer	do	6 "	300 c	" " "	"
103	35	R. H. Sudweeks	Junction	12 "	600 "	" " "	"
104	30	J. H. Dean	Salt Lake City	6 "	300 c	" 27 "	Zane
105	48	Andrew Hansen	West Jordan	18 "	300 c	" " "	"
		Total months & Fine:—		**959**	**$ 32,600**		

48. The middle initial "W" is struck out in pink pencil, and "yumm" is written in pink above it. William Jeffs's middle name was either Yemm or Yumm. (Ancestral File.)

80

No	No	Age	Name	Residence	Term	Fine	Date of Impt.	By whom Sentenced
	85	36	Chas. Denney	Salt Lake City	6 mos	732 26100 300 c	June 1.86	Zane
43	86	44	L. H. Berg	do	6 "	300 c	" 186	"
44	84	49	Jens Hansen	Mill Creek	6 "	300 c	" 2 "	"
45	88	65	Wm Stimpson	Ogden	8 "	300 c	" 5 "	Powers
46	89	54	W. H. Pidcock	do	13 "	---	" 30 "	"
47	90	44	N. H. Groesbeck	Springville	9 "	450 c	Aug 2 "	"
48	91	46	Wm M. Bromley	Am. Fork	10 "	300 c	" 3 "	"
49	92	42	Wm Telsted	Salt Lake City	P. 3 yrs	250 c	Sep. 14 "	Zane
50	93	56	Richd Warburton	Tooele	6 mos	300 c	" 20 "	"
51	94	55	J. E. Lindberg	do	18 "	300 c	" 20 "	"
52	95	58	Wm W. Jeffs	Salt Lake City	19 "	400 c	" 22 "	"
53	96	48	W. W. Galbraith	Kaysville	6 "	300 c	" 22 "	"
54	97	49	Jas Dunn	Tooele	12 "	300 c	" 23 "	"
55	98	45	N. F. Folsom	Salt Lake City	6 "	300 c	" 25 "	"
56	99	55	Wm Robinson	Beaver	6 "	300 c	" 26 "	Boreman
57	100	64	Geo. Hales	do	6 "	300 c	" "	"
58	101	59	Thos Schofield	do	6 "	300 c	" " "	"
59	102	63	Jas. Farrer	do	6 "	300 c	" " "	"
60	103	35	R. H. Sudweeks	Junction	12 "	600 "	" " "	"
	104	30	J. H. Dean	Salt Lake City	6 "	300 c	" 24 "	Zane
	105	48	Andrew Hansen	West Jordan	18 "	300 c	" " "	"
			Total months & Fine:—		959	% 32600		

81

No.	Age	Name	Residence	Term	Fine	Date of Impt	By whom Sentenced
				989	3260o		
107	65	James Higgins	West Jordan	18 mo. 300.		Sept 30 86	Zane
	60	Carl Jensen	do	18 ,	300 c	" 30 ,	"
108	56	John Gillespie	Tooele	6 ,	300 c	" 30 ,	"
109	71	John B. Furster	Salt Lake City	6 ,	300 c	Oct 1 ,	"
110	44	Willard L. Snow	Farmers Ward	18 ,	300 c	" 1 ,	"
111	54	J.H.H. Morton	do	6 ,	300 c	" 1 ,	"
112	53	D.L. Leaker	Salt Lake City	6 ,	300 c	" 6 ,	"
113	42	Isaac R. Pierce	do	15 ,	100 c	" 9 ,	"
114	61	Amos H. Neff	East Mill Creek	12 ,	600 c	" 11 ,	"
115	64	Jas. J. Steel	Tooele Co	12 ,	300 c	" 14 ,	"
116	44	Haus Jensen	Goshen	6 ,	100 c	" 21 ,	Henderson
117	58	Jas. W. Loveless	Provo	6 ,	800 c	" 21 ,	"
118	46	Jno. Durrant	Am. Fk.	6 ,	100 c	" 21 ,	"
119	44	O.P. Arnold	Salt Lake City	15 ,	450 c	" 21 ,	Zane
120	66	John Gray	do	6 ,	50 c	" 30 ,	"
121	46	J. Parkinson	Wellsville	6 ,	100 —	Nov. 23 ,	Henderson
122	63	Geo. Dunford	Salt Lake City	6 ,	150 c	" 24 ,	Zane
123	50	John Stoddard	Ogden	6 ,	300 c	" 29 ,	Henderson
124	44	Lorenzo Stutts	Mill Creek	12 ,	200 c	" " ,	Zane
125	46	M. W. Butter	Ogden	6 ,	100 —	Dec 1 ,	Henderson
126	44	Thos. H Bullock	Salt Creek, mo. C	6 ,	—	" 1 ,	"
		Total months & Fine :—		1154	34500		

No	Age	Name	Residence	Term	Fine	Date of Impt	By whom sentenced
106	65	James Higgins	West Jordan	959 18 mos	32600 300. c	Sept 30 86	Zane
107	60	Carl Jensen	do	18 "	300 c	" 30 "	"
108	56	John Gillespie	Tooele	6 "	300 c.	" 30 "	"
109	71	John B. Furster	Salt Lake City	6 "	300 c	Oct 1 "	"
110	44	Willard L. Snow	Farmers Ward	18 "	300 c	" 1 "	"
111	54	T. H. H. Morton	do	6 "	300 c	" 1 "	"
112	53	D. L. Leaker	Salt Lake City	6 "	300 c	" 6 "	"
113	42	Isaac R. Pierce	do	15 "	100 c	" 9 "	"
114	61	Amos. H. Neff	East Mill Creek	12 "	600 c	" 11 "	"
115	67	Jas. I. Steel	Tooele Co.	12 "	300 c	" 14 "	"
116	44	Hans. Jensen	Goshen	6 "	100 c	" 21 "	Henderson
117	58	Jas. W. Loveless	Provo	6 "	300 c	" 21 "	"
118	46	Jno. Durrant	Am. Fk.	6 "	100 c	" 21 "	"
119	44	O. P. Arnold	Salt Lake City	15 "	450. c	" 21 "	Zane
120	66	John Gray	do	6 "	50 c	" 30 "	"
121	46	T. Parkinson	Wellsville	6 "	100. -	Nov. 23 "	Henderson
122	63	Geo. Dunford	Salt Lake City	6 "	150 c	" 24 "	Zane
123	50	John Stoddard	Ogden	6 "	300 c	" 29 "	Henderson
124	47	Lorenzo Stutts	Mill Creek	12 "	200 c	" " "	Zane
125	46	M. W. Butler	Ogden	6 "	100-	Dec 1 "	Henderson
126	47	Thos. H. Bullock	Salt Creek, Weber Co.	6 "	——	" 1 "	"
			Total months & Fine:—	1154	$ 37500		

[82]

No	Age	Name	Residence	Term	Fine	Date of Impt.	By whom sentenced
127	49	Geo. Naylor	Kamas	1154 6 mos.	37550 300 c	Dec. 3 86	Zane
128	54	Wm Geddes	Plain City	6 "	100	" 6 "	Henderson
129	50	Geo. Chandler	Ogden	6 "	100 c	" 7 "	"
130	40	F. W. Ellis	North Ogden	6 "	100 c	" 13 "	"
131	52	Thos. B. Helm	Pleasant View	6 "	100 c	" 13 "	"
132	54	Jas. May	Calls Fort	6 "	100	" 13 "	"
133	51	H. B. Gwilliam	Hooper	6 "	100 c	" 13 "	"
134	51	Thos. Allsop	Sandy	15 "	50 c	" 14 "	Zane
135	67	Jno. P. Jones	Enoch	6 "	300 c	" 27 "	Boreman
136	44	Jno. Lee Jones	do	6 "	300 c	" 27 "	"
137	28	Jos. H. Thurber	Greenwich	P. 4² yrs	500 c	" 27 "	"
138	45	Peter Petersen	Richville	6 mos.	100 c	" 30 "	Henderson
139	52	Harvey Murdock	Harrisville	P. 5 yrs	500 -	Jan. 3 87	"
140	56	Wm Palmer	Logan	6 mos.	100 -	" 3. 87	"
141	57	Hugh Adams	do	6 "	100 -	" 3 "	"
142	64	Thos. McNeil	do	6 "	100. -	" 3 "	"
143	61	Robt. Henderson	do	6 "	100 -	" 3 "	"
144	52	Peter Anderson	Huntsville	6 "	100 -	" 3 "	"
145	62	Jos. Parry	Ogden	6 "	300 -	" 8 "	"
146	58	Chas Frank	Logan	6 "	100. -	" 8 "	"
147	56	Neils C Mortesen	Huntsville	6 "	300 -	" 8 "	"
		Total months & Fine:—		1394	$ 41400		

No	Age	Name	Residence	Term	Fine	Date of Impt.	By whom sentenced
148	55	Thos. Kirby	Hyde Park	1394 6 mos.	41400 100 -	Jan. 8. 87	Henderson
149	65	Abraham Chadwick	North Ogden	6 "	300 -	" 8. 84	"
150	70	John Marriott	Marriotville	6 "	100 -	" 8 "	"
				1412	41900[48]		

[84]

Feb 18, 1882.

To Roie,
    When you hear the whistle sound
    I'll be there in Brigham-town
    And give you there a bonny gift[49]
    On Saturday—the Twenty-fifth.

    If you'll be good and please Mamma[50]
    And never leave the door ajar
    And ne'er will chase or stone the hens
    Whilst hunting food outside their pens.

    Nor tease, nor plague your sister May
    While you're engaged in mirthful play
    Nor in the carpet drive a nail
    Nor pinch the cat, nor pull Jip's tail—

    Nor take a match to start a fire,
    Of doing right will never tire;
    Do this, my Dearest Little Boy
    And earn the promised, pretty toy.

                              Your Pa,
                                L. Snow.

---

49. The "re" of "there" is struck out in purple pencil, and an "n" is written above, making "then."
50. The word "your" is inserted between "please" and "Mamma" in a bluish-green ink, and "Mamma" is changed to "Ma" by striking out "mma."

84

Feb 18, 1882.

To Rosie,

When you hear the whistle sound
I'll be there in Brigham - town
And give you then a bonny gift -
On Saturday - the Twenty - fifth.

If you'll be good and please your Ma
And never leave the door ajar
And ne'er will chase or stone the hens
Whilst hunting food outside their pens.

Nor tease, nor plague your Sister May
While you're engaged in mirthful play
Nor in the carpet - drive a nail
Nor pinch the cat, nor pull Fifi's tail -

Nor take a match to start a fire,
Of doing right - will never tire:
Do this, my Dearest Little Boy
And earn the promised, pretty toy.
              Your Pa,
                  L. Snow.

85

To Minnie May.

Thy chatty tongue, bewitching smile
With heart so good and free from guile
Thyself as gentle as the dove
When giving Pa thy sweetest love.

Who sometimes awake from midnight-sleep
With kisses pretty, soft and sweet
While little hands steal o'er his face
No less than May's the pure & chaste.

O sweetest-May, I love thee more
Than words can tell or thought explore.
So now, good-bye, my Darling Girl
With smiling face & golden curls.
              Your Pa,
                S. S.
Feb. 20, 1882.

[85]

To Minnie May.
   Thy chatty tongue, bewitching smile
   With heart so good and free from guile
   Thyself as gentle as the dove
   When giving Pa thy sweetest love.

   Who sometimes wake from midnight sleep
   With kisses pretty, soft and sweet
   While little hands steal o'er his face
   No less than May's the pure & chaste.

   O sweetest May, I love thee more
   Than words can tell or thoughts explore.
   So now, good-bye, my Darling Girl
   With smiling face & golden curls.
                    Your Pa,
                      L. S.
Feb. 20, 1882.

[86]
Alviras—Lillie,
  This humble gift you'll please accept
  In token of my love—respect.
  Bound now in <u>one</u> by sacred ties,
  That point aloft beyond the skies
  His blessings choice may God bestow
  On you, Dear Vie and Lillie Snow.
                                Affectionately,
                                  Your Father,
                                  Lorenzo Snow.
Brigham City.

          Lines dedicated to Susa Young Gates
          Editor "Young Womans Journal".⁵¹

---

51. The *Young Woman's Journal* was the official publication of the Church's Young Ladies' National Mutual Improvement Association. Susa Young Gates was its first editor. The *Journal* ran from 1889 to 1929, when it merged with the *Improvement Era*. See Garr, Cannon, and Cowan, *Encyclopedia of Latter-day Saint History*, 1387.

[87]
Brigham City Jan. 1rst, 1892.
Dear Sister Susa:
    The world's ungrateful, always was—
    'Tis needless here to state the cause—
    But she who would true honor gain,
    And tread the path to lasting fame,
    And would be noble, grand and great,
    For generous pay must 'longtime wait;
    Yet struggle hard, and toil and sweat
    And put the world much in her debt:
    But 'way beyond the milky-way
    In life celestial, look for pay.
    And still my Sister Susa Dear
    This work of love you're doing here
    In this degraded, fallen sphere,
    Yet, through our ever blessed Lord
    In <u>this</u> <u>poor</u> <u>life</u> you've <u>some</u> reward.
    He gives thee light and power divine,
    He fires thy heart, inspires thy mind
    With thoughts refined, thoughts choice and grand
    Now wafting o'er fair Zion's land.
    Though golden purse ne'er ope's for thee
    You never shall impov'rished be.
    Let thoughts arise of blessings vast,

[88]
That God bestowed in seasons past;
And ne'er your present state deplore,
Nor fear to sacrifice still more.
To sacrifice and to obey,
Therein do all the honors lay.
Still onward press my Sister Dear
Thy calling's high the prize is near,
And to the end you'll sure endure
And thus as promised, make secure
A glowing, brilliant, sparkling gem—
Celestial, princely, diadem.

Lorenzo Snow. copied by
Minnie J. Snow[52]

Reply

Provo Jan. 6_ 1892.

Pres. Lorenzo Snow,
Dear and kind Brother:—
I can never express to you in words, the grateful, humble feelings that swept over me when I read your beautiful prophecy and poetical consolation. It made me feel so humble, to receive such words from one to whom I have always looked up with feelings of awe and reverence! Oh,

52. The words "copied by Minnie J. Snow" are written on an angle, immediately following "Lorenzo Snow."

[89]

how keenly I felt the force of your lovely words, "Yet through our ever blessed Lord, In this poor life you've some reward". For the friendship and confidence of such men as—'Lorenzo Snow, the President of the Twelve Apostles" I would not exchange the glittering baubles of India or the shining gold of the whole earth. Your inspiration was true when you said, "And ne'er your present state deplore." For this last summer I have suffered intensely over matters connected with the "Journal" and have even ventured to express the wish that the "Journal" had never been started. Ah, let me engrave, in letters of fire upon my heart, these prophetic lines you indicted to me—

"Though golden purse ne'er ope's for thee
You never shall impov'rished be".

And upon my eyelids, let me always see that precious promise "And to the end you'll sure endure.

Dear and kind Friend, as I first said—words are inadequate to express the keen pleasure your letter has given me—I cannot speak my gratitude.

I have asked Sis. E. S. Taylor, and she wishes me to publish this. It may seem egotistical to some, but it is a pleasure I can not deny myself.

[90]

This much I can say—it does not make me feel high-minded or proud, it humbles me in the dust of anxious desire to deserve it all, at some future day.

Once more thanking you, and asking God to prolong your life 'till Zion is Redeemed,

I am your Sister and friend

copied by   Susa Young Gates.

M. J. S.[53]

Apostle Paul to the Philipians;

"Let this mind be in you, which was also in Christ Jesus: Who, being in the form of God, thought it not robbery to be equal with God." (Chap. 2. Verse 5–6 St. Paul.)

Dear Brother:

Hast thou not been unwisely bold
Man's destiny to thus unfold
To raise, promote such high desire,
Such vast ambition thus inspire?

Still: 'tis no phantom that we trace
Man's ultimatum in life's race;
This royal path has long been trod
By righteous men, who now are Gods:

---

53. The words "copied by M. J. S" are on an angle and circled.

As Abram, Isaac, Jacob too,
First babes, then men, to Gods they grew;
As man now is, our God once was
As now God is, so man may be,[54]

Which fact unfolds man's destiny.
So John asserts; "When Christ we see
Then we like him will truly be,
And he, this hope, who has in him

Will purify himself from sin."[55]
This object grand who keep in view,
To folly, sin, will bid adieu,
Nor wallow in this mire anew,

Nor ever seek to graft his name
High on the spire of worldly fame;
But here his ultimatum trace—
The head of all his spirit-race.

Ah, well: that taught by you Dear Paul,
'Though much amazed, we see it all;
Our Father God, has ope'd our eyes,
So cannot view it otherwise.

---

54. See note 17.
55. See 1 John 3:2–3.

[92]

The boy who like his father's grown
He's taken only what's his own;
When son of man has man become
He 'gainst no law of nature run.

A son of God like God to be
Would not be robbing Deity
"And he who has this hope in him
Will purify himself of sin.[56]

You're right St. John, supremely right
Who e'er essays to climb this height
Will cleanse himself of sin entire
Or else 'twere needless to aspire.

Lorenzo Snow.

Brigham Jan. 11, 1892.   M. J. S.[57]

---

56. See 1 John 3:3.
57. "M. J. S." is on an angle.

Brigham—Aug. 31ʳˢᵗ, 1891.

    Minnie J. Snow:

How sweet are the thoughts, when, once and for all,
We promised to love, and never recall.[58]
And sweet loving times so oft repeated,
Heave welded our hearts, nor love yet abated.
Untarnished our love, still brighter its glow,
As two streamlets unite, then together they flow.
Right well hast thou love'd, and bravely hast trod,
The path He appointed—Our Father and God;
And wond'rously blest, in mind and in heart
Your fame's been extended–shall never depart.
But constant and blazoned with glory, renown,
'Till thou a bright Queen and Goddess be crowned.

Oft have I viewed thee, rise and address,
Truths of high import, thy Sister to bless;
As an angel of light, teaching with power,
The very thing needed, for the day and the hour;
Inspiring the heart, enlightening the mind
In style most sublime and el'quence refined.

Thy fruitful mind and talents rare
And gift of heart—a gracious share—

---

58. Minnie Jensen and Lorenzo Snow were married in the Endowment House in Salt Lake City on June 12, 1871.

[94]
Art kind and gentle—good to all,
Responding to each public call,
Supressing self, when self appears,
Be it roses, thorns or tears.
And thus continue—thus be great,
'Till God, the Son, Shall come in state

                                        Lorenzo.

Written for our friends assembled to celebrate our Twentieth Wedding Anniversary. June 12, 1891.
        To our Friends, Greeting.
All hail, sweet friends, right welcome here
It warms our heart to feel you're near;
Such taste and intellect refined
And gifts of heart in you combined
Spread light—give joy in our abode
This rare, this precious episode.
This pleasing style, this unique way
You celebrate our nuptial day
Delight our heart, high honor's shed
Upon that happy day we wed.

[95]

[Blank]

[96]

Brigham Jan. 1rst, 1892

Dear George and Lana:
    That golden pen with diamond point
    With holder fine is nicely wrought,
    With cushion too, so sweet and chaste
    Its donor I could easy trace—
    A priceless gift—a present rare
    That indicates, your love I share.
    But other Christmas days have told
    Your love for me had not grown cold.
    And now my Son and Daughter too
    To bear my thanks, (I feel its due)
    This missive, Dears, to send to you.
    May blessings choice forever flow
    Enrich your labors here below,
    Infuse your heart with holy fire
    And sanctify each thought, desire,
    That 'way beyond high ether blue
    In realms of light, where both of you
    May there be crowned a King, a Queen
    By our great Father—Elohiem.

Affectionately Your Father
Lorenzo Snow.

M.J.S.

[97]

To Le Roi C. Snow and Companion F. Olsen while on a mission to Germany.

Mar. 3, 1897.

To you my Son, Dear Olsen too
I rhyme these thoughts and send to you.
You need not look for only rhyme
With thoughts but couch'd in jingling line.

Dear Olsen's had experience more
And taught in school scholastic lore,
Thy senior too he stands confess'd
With which no doubt thou art impress'd.

Let no envious feelings rise
To ruffle friendship's tender ties
No thoughts or words but pure & kind.
Let love prevail in heart and mind
Like Jonathan and David be
That your sweet union Saints may see
And worship God and honor thee
Be one in heart be one in thought

[98]
A principle our Savior taught.[59]
While two unite in mission work
No one should show a wish to shirk
But take the humbler part e'en more

'Though he might feel a little sore.
And, thus his pride must lay aside
God's lowly spirit be his guide
O'er his passions triumphant ride.

Very Affectionately
Lorenzo Snow.
S. L. Temple.

---

59. See John 17:11, 21–22.

98

A principle our Savior taught:
While two unite in mission work
No one should show a wish to shirk
But take the humbler part e'en more

Though he might feel a little sore.
And thus his pride must lay aside
God's lowly spirit be his guide
O'er his passions triumphant ride.
    Very Affectionately
        Lorenzo Snow.
        S. L. Temple.

99

Elder George Bywater,
Expressive of my love to thee
This token please accept of me
His blessings choice may God bestow
On thee dear friend, while here below
With roses fair thy path bestrew
That never tire in charming you
'Cause thou art noble, good and great
As wast thou in thy first estate
                Affectionately
                        Lorenzo Snow.
June 2nd 1896.
        On J. S. Sec.

Elder George Bywater:
Expressive of my love to thee
This token please accept of me
His blessings choice may God bestow
On thee Dear friend, while here below
With roses fair thy path bestrew
That never tire in charming you
'Cause thou art noble, good and great
As wast thou in thy first estate

Affectionately
Lorenzo Snow.

June 2ᵃⁿᵈ 1896.
M. J. S. Sec.

[pages 100–224 blank]

APPENDIX

Individuals Mentioned in the Record Book

Isabel Ball was born October 14, 1872, in Salt Lake City to John Price Ball and Phoebe Birkenhead.[1] She married James W. Ure Jr. on June 25, 1895, in Salt Lake City.[2] Isabel died January 17, 1906.[3]

John Price Ball was born October 4, 1828, in Coalville, Leicestershire, England, to James Ball and Isabel Price. Ball married Emma Henderson April 2, 1859, in Loughborough, England.[4] Ball married Phobe Birkenhead on March 4, 1870, in Salt Lake City.[5] On November 7, 1885, he was arrested on the charge of unlawful cohabitation[6] and on February 27, 1886, was sentenced by Judge Zane to six months' imprisonment and a $300 fine.[7] When his prison sentence was up on August 30, 1886, Ball was not released from the penitentiary with others whose sentences

1. Frank Esshom, *Pioneers and Prominent Men of Utah* (Salt Lake City: Western Epics, 1966), 733.
2. Esshom, *Pioneers and Prominent Men*, 733; Salt Lake County Clerk. *Record of Marriage Licenses, Books E–G, 1893–1897* (Salt Lake City: Genealogical Society of Utah, 1965) microfilm 429056, license no. 5030.
3. Ancestral File.
4. Esshom, *Pioneers and Prominent Men*, 732.
5. Esshom, *Pioneers and Prominent Men*, 733.
6. Andrew Jenson, *Church Chronology: A Record of Important Events Pertaining to the History of the Church of Jesus Christ of Latter-day Saints*, 2nd ed. (Salt Lake City: Deseret News, 1914), 125.
7. Jenson, *Church Chronology*, 129.

had been served, because he declined to pay his fine.[8] He died October 16, 1890, in Salt Lake City.[9]

Samuel Frederick Ball was born April 14, 1849, in Stockcross, Berkshire, England, to Samuel Leonard Ball and Hannah Maria Marshall.[10] He married Margaret Poiney March 23, 1873, in Brighton, England.[11] Ball later married Ellen (Nellie) Maria Powell and Margaret Brown. Ball's Church service included president of the Lambeth Branch in the England conference, patriarch of the Salt Lake Stake,[12] president of the Second Quorum of the Seventy, first counselor to Bishop Theodore McKean in the Twenty-ninth Ward, member of President George Q. Cannon's prayer circle, and superintendent of Sunday School in the Twenty-second Ward.[13] He was arrested January 6, 1886, on the charge of unlawful cohabitation[14] and on March 1, 1886, was sentenced by Judge Zane to six months in prison and a $300 fine.[15] Ball was released from the penitentiary September 4, 1886.[16] He died December 13, 1923, in Salt Lake City.[17]

William Green Bickley was born May 1, 1842, in Small Hill, England, to parents Samuel Bickley and Mary Green.[18] He came to Utah in 1862 and eventually settled in Minersville, Beaver

8. Jenson, *Church Chronology*, 136.
9. Jenson, *Church Chronology*, 188.
10. Andrew Jenson, *Latter-day Saint Biographical Encyclopedia: A Compilation of Biographical Sketches of Prominent Men and Women in the Church of Jesus Christ of Latter-day Saints* (Salt Lake City: Andrew Jenson History Company, 1901–35), 3:10.
11. Jenson, *Biographical Encyclopedia*, 10.
12. Fawn Pace Burt, *The First Sixty Years of the Twenty-ninth Ward in Salt Lake City* (Salt Lake City: n.p., 1964), 114.
13. Jenson, *LDS Biographical Encyclopedia*, 10.
14. Jenson, *Church Chronology*, 127.
15. Jenson, *Church Chronology*, 129.
16. Jenson, *Church Chronology*, 136.
17. Burt, *First Sixty Years*, 115.
18. United States 1880 Federal Census, Beaver County, Utah, 5; Ancestral File; "W. G. Bickley, Useful and Busy Man, Dies," *Deseret Evening News*, August 17, 1917, 10.

County.[19] Bickley married Jane Walton on March 21, 1867, in Pine Valley, Utah.[20] His occupation in Beaver was music leader.[21] Bickley was arrested May 15, 1886, on the charge of unlawful cohabitation and on May 27, 1886, was sentenced to six months in prison and a $300 fine.[22] He was released from the penitentiary November 29, 1886.[23] He died August 9, 1917, in Beaver, Utah.[24]

Melissa (or Malissa) Canfield Borlase was born August 26, 1852, in Ogden, Utah, to parents Cyrus C. Canfield and Clarissa Jones.[25] Mrs. Borlase married Rawsel Bradford on July 17, 1869, and later she married John Borlase about 1878 in Utah.[26] Mrs. Borlase died February 10, 1912, in Salt Lake City.[27] Her duties in the Church included offices in the Sunday School and Relief Society. She died February 10, 1912, in Midvale, Utah.[28]

John Bowen was born September 12, 1841, in Abersychan, Monmouth, Wales, to Lewis Bowen and Mary Ann Harris.[29] He came to the United States in 1862 to join his brother, David. Together they worked to earn money to bring the rest of the family to Utah.[30] In 1863 Bowen moved with his family to Tooele, Utah. He married Hannah Johnson in January 1877. He also

---

19. "W. G. Bickley," 10.
20. United States 1880 Federal Census, Beaver County, Utah, 5.
21. Ancestral File.
22. Jenson, *Church Chronology*, 132–33.
23. Jenson, *Church Chronology*, 141.
24. Ancestral File; "W. G. Bickley," 10.
25. "Well Known Woman Dies: Mrs. Melissa Borlase Mourned by Many Throughout State," *Deseret News*, February 1912, 3; United States 1880 Federal Census, Salt Lake County, Utah, 305.
26. Ancestral File.
27. Jenson, *Church Chronology*, 50.
28. "Well Known Woman Dies," 3.
29. Tooele County Daughters of Utah Pioneers, *History of Tooele County* (Salt Lake City: Publishers Press, 1961), 427.
30. *History of Tooele County*, 427.

married Eliza Elizabeth Craner on October 10, 1880.[31] Bowen was arrested on the charges of polygamy and unlawful cohabitation July 16, 1885.[32] On February 17, 1886, he was sentenced to six months in prison and a $300 fine. He was taken to the penitentiary that afternoon[33] and was released August 20, 1886.[34] He died September 20, 1922, in Tooele, Utah.[35]

Rosena Singleton Bromley was born April 17, 1852, in Portsmouth, England, to Francis Singleton and Amelia Ann Williams.[36] She came to America with her parents in 1864. They arrived in Utah November 4, 1864, with the Warren Snow company.[37] She married William Michael Bromley July 19, 1870, in Salt Lake City.[38] Mrs. Bromley died February 25, 1918, in American Fork, Utah.[39]

William Michael Bromley was born October 13, 1839, in Worcester, England, to John Bromley and Mary Oxenbold. William left for America with his family in 1851 and arrived in Utah by himself (due to the deaths of family members) in 1855. He settled in Springfield, Utah, where he worked as a blacksmith, farmer, and bookkeeper. He married Elizabeth Roylance November 10, 1858, in Springville, Utah. He later married three other women: Rosena Singleton on July 19, 1870, in Salt Lake City, Caroline Whiting in 1879 in Salt Lake City, and Beulah Chipman in March 1885 in American Fork, Utah.[40] Bromley was arrested on January 11, 1886, on the charge of unlawful cohabitation[41]

---

31. *History of Tooele County*, 428.
32. Jenson, *Church Chronology*, 122.
33. Jenson, *Church Chronology*, 129.
34. Jenson, *Church Chronology*, 135.
35. *History of Tooele County*, 428.
36. Esshom, *Pioneers and Prominent Men*, 771.
37. Esshom, *Pioneers and Prominent Men*, 771.
38. Esshom, *Pioneers and Prominent Men*, 771.
39. "Mrs. Bromley Dies of Paralytic Stroke," *Deseret Evening News*, February 26, 1918, 4.
40. Esshom, *Pioneers and Prominent Men*, 771.
41. Jenson, *Church Chronology*, 127.

and on April 13, 1886, was sentenced to ten months in prison and a $300 fine.[42] He entered the penitentiary August 3, 1886,[43] and was released February 9, 1887.[44] He died April 14, 1914, in American Fork, Utah.[45]

Thomas Burningham was born to Thomas Burningham and Sarah White. He came to Utah by 1861. Burningham married Ellen Hook in 1861 in Bountiful, Utah. He later married Lucina Sessions. Burningham's Church service included being a ward teacher and high priest, serving a mission to England, and acting as a member of the Seventieth Quorum of Seventies.[46] He was "arrested on a trumped up charge of threatening to kill, brought to Salt Lake, and charged with unlawful cohabitation" on July 17, 1885.[47] He was pronounced guilty of unlawful cohabitation on February 10, 1886, and was sentenced to six months in prison and a $300 fine on February 17, 1886.[48] Burningham was released from the penitentiary August 20, 1886.[49] He died in 1893 in Salt Lake City.[50]

Maria Burrows was born November 5, 1870, in Nottingham, England.[51] She was the daughter of Elisabeth Holmes and William Burrows and came to Utah with them in 1872.[52] She married Franklin Crow (the son of Charles Henry Crow and

42. Jenson, *Church Chronology*, 131.
43. Jenson, *Church Chronology*, 135.
44. Jenson, *Church Chronology*, 143.
45. Esshom, *Pioneers and Prominent Men*, 771.
46. Esshom, *Pioneers and Prominent Men*, 783.
47. Jensen, *Church Chronology*, 122.
48. Jensen, *Church Chronology*, 128–29.
49. Jensen, *Church Chronology*, 135.
50. Esshom, *Pioneers and Prominent Men*, 783.
51. The Church of Jesus Christ of Latter-day Saints, *Granite Stake Genealogical Survey, 1920–1924* (Salt Lake City: Genealogical Society of Utah, 1950), microfilm 368515.
52. Esshom, *Pioneers and Prominent Men*, 830.

Mary Sharp) on September 12, 1894, in Salt Lake City.[53] She was honored as Utah's first war mother when her son Raymond Crow was killed in action in France, the first Utahn to lose his life in World War I. She was also a charter member of the Utah Chapter, Gold Star Mothers and a member of the Service Star Legion for many years. She and her husband were the parents of six children, five of which lived to adulthood.[54] She was a resident of Salt Lake City for over sixty years and died at her home in Los Angeles on December 31, 1950.[55]

There are two possible George Bywaters. The only ones found were father and son:

1. **George Gwilym Bywater** was born November 15, 1828, in Bedwelty, Wales, to George Henry Bywater and Elinor Gwillym. He married Martha Jones, the daughter of Rees Rees Jones and Martha Phillips, on November 27, 1854, in Salt Lake City. George and Martha were the parents of seven children, all born in Salt Lake City. Bywater served as a teacher in his ward, as president of a quorum of seventy, and as a missionary.[56] He died May 16, 1898, in Salt Lake City.[57]

2. **George Jones Bywater** was born November 10, 1855, in Salt Lake City to George Gwilym Bywater and Martha Jones. He married Jeannette Russell Yeates, the daughter of William Yeates and Margaret Fife, on July 28, 1856, in Salt Lake City. George and Jeannette were the parents of six children, born in

---

53. Salt Lake County Clerk, *Record of Marriage Licenses, Books E–G, 1893–1897* (Salt Lake: Genealogical Society of Utah, 1965), microfilm 429056, no. 4471; Esshom, *Pioneers and Prominent Men*, 830.
54. Esshom, *Pioneers and Prominent Men*, 830.
55. "Funeral Rites Set Friday for Mrs. Crow," *Deseret News*, January 2, 1951, 4B.
56. "Elder George G. Bywater: Funeral Services Held in the Salt Lake Stake Assembly Hall," *Deseret Evening News*, May 20, 1898, 5.
57. Ancestral File.

Logan and Salt Lake City. George died November 6, 1899, in Salt Lake City.[58]

John Thomas Caine was born January 8, 1829, on the Isle of Man, Parish of Kirkpatrick, England, to Thomas Caine and Elinor Cubbon.[59] In 1846 Caine immigrated to the United States. He married Margaret Nightengale October 28, 1850, in St. Louis, Missouri. Caine and his family made the trip to Utah and arrived in Salt Lake September 20, 1852.[60] He also became involved in politics and held the positions of, among others, territorial and state legislator, territorial delegate in Congress, member of the Constitutional Convention of 1882, and member of House of Representatives in 1883.[61] Later, after retiring from Congress in 1893, Caine was auditor of accounts for Utah Territory and superintendent of waterworks for Salt Lake City. He was also one of the original stockholders and directors of Zion's Savings Bank and Trust Company as well as the director, secretary, and treasurer of the Joseph Agricultural and Stock Company. Caine's Church service included a mission to the Sandwich Islands, where he was a counselor to the mission president, Silas Smith, as well as callings as a teacher and high counselor.[62] He died September 20, 1911, in Salt Lake City.[63]

Abraham Hoagland Cannon was born March 12, 1859, in Salt Lake City to George Q. Cannon and Elizabeth Hoagland.[64] Cannon married four times. His first marriage was to Sarah A. Jenkins. He later married Wilhelmina M. Cannon, Mary Croxall, and

58. "Death of Geo. J. Bywater: Well Known Actor and Artist Passed Away in This City Today," *Deseret Evening News*, November 6, 1899, 2.
59. Kate B. Carter, *Our Pioneer Heritage* (Salt Lake City: Daughters of Utah Pioneers, 1958), 16:519.
60. Carter, *Our Pioneer Heritage*, 520.
61. Orson F. Whitney, *History of Utah* (Salt Lake City: George Q. Cannon, 1904), 675.
62. Esshom, *Pioneers and Prominent Men*, 789–90.
63. Jenson, *Church Chronology*, 38.
64. Jenson, *LDS Biographical Encyclopedia*, 167.

Lillian Hamblin.[65] Cannon was involved in many companies in Utah. Some of the positions he held included director of the State Bank of Utah, director of the Utah Loan and Trust Company, director of ZCMI, and director of the Co-Operative Furniture Company.[66] He also worked closely with the *Juvenile Instructor*, the *Contributor*, and the *Deseret News*.[67] He was arrested April 28, 1885, on the charge of unlawful cohabitation and was placed under a $1,500 bond.[68] On March 17, 1886, Cannon was sentenced to six months in prison and a $300 fine.[69] He was released from the penitentiary August 17, 1886.[70] He died July 19, 1896, in Salt Lake City, at thirty-seven years of age.[71]

Alice Cannon was born January 11, 1882, in Salt Lake City to Angus M. and Cordelia Moses Cannon.[72] She married Joseph LeRoy Cheney on November 14, 1906, in Salt Lake City. Her Church service included working in the Relief Society and callings as Primary president and Sunday School teacher. Alice Cannon Cheney died March 18, 1967, in Centerville, Utah.[73]

Leonora M. Cannon was born to Sarah Maria Mousley and Angus M. Cannon on October 2, 1874, in Salt Lake City.[74] On September 13, 1899, Miss Cannon married Barnard J. Stewart in Salt Lake City.[75] She was one of the first students at LDS

65. Esshom, *Pioneers and Prominent Men*, 793.
66. Jenson, *LDS Biographical Encyclopedia*, 168.
67. Lawrence R. Flake, *Mighty Men of Zion: General Authorities of the Last Dispensation* (Salt Lake City: Karl D. Butler, 1974), 235.
68. Jenson, *Church Chronology*, 120.
69. Jenson, *Church Chronology*, 130.
70. Jenson, *Church Chronology*, 135.
71. Jenson, *LDS Biographical Encyclopedia*, 168.
72. Obituary of Alice C. Cheney, *Deseret News*, March 20, 1967, B11.
73. Marriage License of Alice Cannon and Joseph L. Cheney, Salt Lake County, Book 4, page 113, November 14, 1906; Obituary, B11.
74. "Mrs. Stewart, Civic Worker, Dies at 86," *Deseret News and Telegram*, March 25, 1961, 14A.
75. Certificate of Marriage, Barnard J. Stewart to Leonora M. Cannon, September 9, 1899, Salt Lake County, Utah, Book I, 499, Microfilm 429035.

University and attended the University of Utah. She served as president of the University Ward Relief Society and in the Ensign Stake Relief Society presidency. Leonora Cannon Stewart died September 24, 1961, in Salt Lake City.[76]

Wilhelmina Mousley Cannon was born July 23, 1859, in Salt Lake City, the oldest daughter of Angus M. Cannon, an early Church official, and Ann Amanda Cannon. She was married first to Abraham Hoagland Cannon of the Council of the Twelve. He died in 1896 and she married Fred Arden Ellis January 17, 1901, in Ogden, Utah.[77] Wilhelmina Cannon Ellis died October 6, 1941, in Salt Lake City.[78]

Lydia Spencer Clawson was born on November 13, 1860, in Utah to Daniel Spencer and Mary Jane Cutcliffe.[79] She married Rudger Clawson March 29, 1883 (the marriage card says October 26, 1887), in Salt Lake City, Utah, as his second wife.[80] On October 24, 1884, Lydia was arrested and sent to the Utah Penitentiary because she refused to testify in her husband's trial for unlawful cohabitation. The next day, October 25, 1884, she admitted to being Rudger Clawson's wife. Minutes after she confessed, the jury "returned a verdict of guilty against [Rudger] Clawson."[81] Mrs. Clawson died February 1, 1941, in Salt Lake City.[82]

76. "Mrs. Stewart, Civic Worker, Dies at 86," 14A.
77. "Mrs. Ellis Dies at Home," *Deseret News*, October 7, 1941, 5; Certificate of Marriage, Fred A. Ellis to Mina Cannon, January 17, 1901, Salt Lake County, Utah, Book B, 297.
78. "Mrs. Ellis Dies at Home," 5.
79. "Funeral Is Set for Mrs. Clawson," *Deseret News*, February 3, 1941, 1, 3; United States 1900 Federal Census, Salt Lake County, Utah, ED# 39, p. 5, line 67; Salt Lake Eighteenth Ward, *Membership Records, 1883–1902* (Salt Lake City: Genealogical Society of Utah, 1951, microfilm 26740), 394.
80. Ralph B. Simmons, *Utah's Distinguished Personalities: A Biographical Directory of Eminent Contemporaneous Men and Women Who are the Faithful Builders and Defenders of the State* (Salt Lake City: Personality Publishing Company, 1933), 1:79.
81. Jenson, *Church Chronology*, 116.
82. "Funeral Is Set for Mrs. Clawson," 3–4.

Rudger Clawson was born March 12, 1857, in Salt Lake City, Utah, to Hiram Brandley Clawson and Margaret Gay Judd.[83] He married Florence A. Dinwoodey in 1882 in Salt Lake City. He later married Lydia Spencer on March 29, 1883, in Salt Lake City.[84] Clawson served in the Quorum of the Twelve Apostles from October 10, 1898, until his death.[85] He was also sustained as Second Counselor to President Lorenzo Snow on October 6, 1901, but was never set apart due to the death of President Snow four days later.[86] Additionally, Clawson served as Acting President of the Quorum of the Twelve Apostles from June 1, 1919, to March 2, 1921, and as President of the Twelve Apostles from March 17, 1921, until his death.[87] Clawson was arrested April 24, 1884, on the charge of polygamy and was placed under bonds of $3,000.[88] Clawson's trial began October 15, 1884, and continued for six days. However, since the jury could not agree on a decision, they were discharged and preparations were made for a new trial. On October 24, 1884, Clawson's second wife, Lydia, was arrested and taken to the Utah Penitentiary because she refused to testify at her husband's trial. She was released from prison the following day when she admitted to being Clawson's wife. After Lydia's confession, Rudger Clawson was declared guilty of polygamy and was sentenced to four years in prison and an $800 fine.[89] While he was in prison, Clawson's first wife, Florence Dinwoodey, divorced him on July 25, 1885.[90] He was released from the penitentiary December 12, 1887, after being pardoned by the President of the United States, Grover

---

83. Jenson, *LDS Biographical Encyclopedia*, 174.
84. Simmons, *Utah's Distinguished Personalities*, 79.
85. Jenson, *LDS Biographical Encyclopedia*, 178.
86. Lawrence R. Flake, *Mighty Men of Zion: General Authorities of the Last Dispensation* (Salt Lake City: Karl D. Butler, 1974), 131.
87. Simmons, *Utah's Distinguished Personalities*, 79.
88. Jenson, *Church Chronology*, 114.
89. Jenson, *Church Chronology*, 116–17.
90. Jenson, *Church Chronology*, 123.

Cleveland.[91] Clawson was imprisoned a total of three years, one month, and ten days.[92] He died June 21, 1943.[93]

Grover Cleveland was born March 13, 1837, in Caldwell, New Jersey,[94] to Richard Falley Cleveland and Anne Neal.[95] He married Frances Folsom June 2, 1886.[96] Cleveland worked as an attorney until 1884 and held positions such as sheriff of Erie County, mayor of Buffalo, and governor of New York.[97] In 1884 he ran as the Democratic candidate for president of the United States and won. He served his first term from 1885 to 1888. He served his second term as president from 1893 to 1896.[98] After his service as president, Cleveland wrote and did consulting. He also became a trustee of Princeton University. He died June 24, 1908, in Princeton, New Jersey.[99]

William James Cox was born June 19, 1815, in Nashville, Utah.[100] He was one of the first Latter-day Saints to colonize San Bernardino, California, in 1851.[101] After this area was established he returned to Utah and settled in Beaver, Utah.[102] His Church service included callings such as high councilor, San Bernardino Branch president, and a member of the Twenty-second Quorum of the Seventy. Cox also held a seat in the House of Representatives beginning in 1862.[103] He was married March 3,

91. Jenson, *Church Chronology*, 156.
92. Flake, *Mighty Men of Zion*, 131.
93. Flake, *Mighty Men of Zion*, 130.
94. Rexford G. Tugwell, *Grover Cleveland* (New York: Macmillan, 1968), xiii.
95. Allan Nevins, *Grover Cleveland: A Study in Courage* (New York: Dodd, Mead & Company, 1962), picture titled "Grover Cleveland's Parents," n.p.
96. Tugwell, *Grover Cleveland*, xvi.
97. Tugwell, *Grover Cleveland*, xiv–xv.
98. Tugwell, *Grover Cleveland*, xv–xviii.
99. Tugwell, *Grover Cleveland*, xviii.
100. Lorenzo Snow to W. J. Cox, October 16, 1886: "Dear Bro: Sweet smiling June of Eighty seven Will mark thee sixty one and seven . . . "; Ancestral File.
101. Carter, *Our Pioneer Heritage*, 476.
102. Carter, *Our Pioneer Heritage*, 477.
103. Carter, *Our Pioneer Heritage*, 476–77.

1851, to Delilah Forrester or Forrest. He married a second wife, Josephine Willis, July 21, 1860, in Beaver, Utah; a third wife, Elizabeth Entwhistle, on October 4, 1862; and a fourth wife, Mary Ann Forrester or Forrest, on October 28, 1872.[104] Cox was arrested on the charge of unlawful cohabitation in April 1886.[105] On May 27, 1886, he was sentenced to six months in prison and a $300 fine.[106] Cox was discharged from the Utah Penitentiary on November 29, 1886.[107]

Elizabeth Ann (or Lizzie) Cutler was born June 22, 1861, to Harmon Cutler and Lucy Ann Pettigrew.[108] She was a public school teacher.[109] She married Aaron Henry Williams September 7, 1894, in Salt Lake City.[110] Lizzie died in Idaho about June 1914.[111]

Charles Denney was born on August 11, 1849, in London, Middlesex County, England, to Charles Denny and Mary Ann Dangerfield.[112] He was baptized at age nine and immigrated to the United States in 1866. Denney married Sarah Ann Gold in 1872 in Utah. He also married Lucy Flowers in 1876, although they agreed to separate after he served in the Penitentiary for unlawful cohabitation. He worked at the *Deseret News* as a typesetter. Denney's Church service included positions as choir leader, secretary of the YMMIA, assistant secretary to Beekeepers Society, and a member of the Quorum of the Seventy.[113]

---

104. Ancestral File.
105. Jenson, *Church Chronology*, 131.
106. Jenson, *Church Chronology*, 133.
107. Jenson, *Church Chronology*, 141.
108. Esshom, *Pioneers and Prominent Men*, 833.
109. "Lizzie Cutler Williams: An Appreciation," *Deseret News*, July 4, 1914, 12.
110. Marriage Certificate of Aaron Henry Williams and Elizabeth Ann Cutler, September 27, 1894, Salt Lake County Clerk, license number 4647.
111. "Lizzie Cutler Williams," 12.
112. Davis Bitton, *Guide to Mormon Diaries and Autobiographies* (Provo, UT: Brigham Young University Press, 1930), 88; "Denney Rites Are Arranged," *Deseret News*, September 13, 1937, 12.
113. Bitton, *Guide to Mormon Diaries*, 88.

He was arrested April 17, 1886, for unlawful cohabitation and placed under $1,000 bond.[114] On June 1, 1886, He was sentenced to six months in prison and a $300 fine.[115] He was released from the penitentiary December 1, 1886. He died September 11, 1937, in Murray, Utah.[116]

Francis Hilliard Dyer, also known as Frank or Marshal Dyer, was born September 5, 1854, in Yazoo City, Mississippi, to parents Frank B. and Winifred S. Dyer.[117] He arrived in Salt Lake City April 6, 1876, and on July 8, 1880, married Ellen F. Tavey, with whom he had three children. President Grover Cleveland appointed Dyer as U.S. Marshal for the Utah Territory on April 12, 1886, and he received his commission on June 16 that same year. On November 7, 1887, he was appointed by the Supreme Court of Utah to be the receiver of confiscated Church property for the federal government during the Edmunds-Tucker Act. Marshal Frank Dyer was not active in religion but played an active role in politics as a Democrat. He died March 25, 1892, in Salt Lake City.[118]

Hyrum Pearse Folsom was born September 1, 1841, in Buffalo, New York, to parents William Harrison Folsom and Zerviah Eliza Clark. He married Nancy Broadbent December 29, 1866, in Salt Lake City. He married a second wife, Annie Eliza Lenzi, on January 4, 1879, in Salt Lake City.[119] He was imprisoned for unlawful cohabitation on September 25, 1886, and was released

114. Jenson, *Church Chronology*, 131.
115. Jenson, *Church Chronology*, 133.
116. "Lizzie Cutler Williams," 12.
117. Whitney, Orson F., *History of Utah* (Salt Lake City: George Q. Cannon & Sons, 1904), 4:281–82.
118. Whitney, *History of Utah*, 281–82: "Death of Frank H. Dyer," *Deseret Evening News*, March 26, 1892, 5.
119. Esshom, *Pioneers and Prominent Men*, 874.

February 24, 1887, with a $300 fine.[120] He died September 23, 1924, in Salt Lake City.[121]

Herbert John Foulger was born January 10, 1848, in Islington, London, England, to John Foulger and Susannah Woolnough. Foulger arrived in Utah October 3, 1863, with the Daniel McArthur company. Foulger married Eliza Mary Hazel April 24, 1871.[122] He was arrested October 31, 1885, on the charge of unlawful cohabitation. November 7, 1885, Foulger pled not guilty to the charge and was placed under $3,500 bonds.[123] On February 11, 1883, he was pronounced guilty of unlawful cohabitation and on February 26 was sentenced to six months in prison and a $300 fine.[124] He was not released from prison with others on August 30, 1886, because he had not paid his fine, which he "declined to do." Foulger was released from the penitentiary September 2, 1886.[125] He died December 6, 1920, in Salt Lake City.[126]

Delila Rebecca Gardner was born June 28, 1878, in Spanish Fork, Utah, to Neil Gardner and Helene Regina Evensen.[127] She married Joseph Hughes, the son of Morgan Hughes and Hannah David, on August 14, 1901, in Salt Lake City. They were the parents of nine children. Delila taught school in Spanish Fork before she married. She served in the Church as a Sunday School teacher, as a member of the Stake Primary Board, as ward Relief

120. Stan Larson, ed., *Prisoner for Polygamy* (Chicago: University of Illinois, 1993), 217.
121. "Hyrum Folsom, Pioneer of 60's Dies at His Home," *Deseret News*, September 24, 1924, 8.
122. Esshom, *Pioneers and Prominent Men*, 876.
123. Jenson, *Church Chronology*, 125.
124. Jenson, *Church Chronology*, 128–29.
125. Jenson, *Church Chronology*, 136.
126. "Hyrum Folsom, Pioneer of 60's Dies at His Home," 8.
127. The Church of Jesus Christ of Latter-day Saints, *Genealogical Surveys of L.D.S. Members: Autobiographies and Ancestors, 1924–1929* microfilm (Salt Lake City: Genealogical Society of Utah, 1977), 542.

Society president, and as stake Relief Society president.[128] She died September 21, 1955, in Spanish Fork, Utah.[129]

Susa Young Gates was born March 18, 1856, in Salt Lake City, Utah, to Brigham Young and Lucy Bigelow.[130] She married Jacob F. Gates in 1880.[131] Her writing was published in the *Deseret News, Juvenile Instructor, Women's Exponent,* and *Young Woman's Journal.* She submitted much of her writing under the pen name Homespun.[132] Susa taught theology, domestic science, and music at the Brigham Young Academy. She also accompanied her husband on a four-year mission to the Sandwich Islands from 1885 to 1889. In 1911 she was appointed to the General Board of Relief Societies.[133] Mrs. Gates died May 27, 1933, in Salt Lake City.[134]

Hyrum Goff was born July 29, 1849, in Longwhatton, Leicestershire, England, to Isaac Goff and Mary Naylor. Goff married Maria T. Arnold January 2, 1871. He later married Marinda P. Bateman on October 24, 1878, in Salt Lake City. His community service included being the first mayor of Midvale, Utah, in 1909.[135] Goff was ordained to the office of the Quorum of the Seventy on January 3, 1877. Goff was also a member of the presidency of the Thirty-third Quorum of the Seventy from 1887 to 1891, first counselor in the bishopric of the West Jordan Ward from 1891 to 1895, bishop of the East Jordan Ward in 1895, and President of the Jordan Stake from 1900 to 1901.[136] Goff was arrested on January 13, 1886, on the charge of unlawful cohab-

128. *Genealogical Surveys of L.D.S. Members,* 542.
129. Obituary of Delilah G. Hughes, *Deseret News,* September 23, 1955, B11.
130. Jenson, *LDS Biographical Encyclopedia,* 626.
131. Jenson, *LDS Biographical Encyclopedia,* 627.
132. Jenson, *LDS Biographical Encyclopedia,* 626–29.
133. Jenson, *LDS Biographical Encyclopedia,* 629.
134. "Susa Y. Gates, Church Worker and Writer Dies," *Deseret News,* May 27, 1933, 1.
135. Esshom, *Pioneers and Prominent Men,* 893.
136. Jenson, *LDS Biographical Encyclopedia,* 309.

itation and taken to Salt Lake City.[137] On February 16, 1886, Goff was declared guilty of polygamy, and on March 3, 1886, he was sentenced to six months in prison and a $300 fine.[138] On September 7, 1886, Goff completed his required prison sentence, was taken to Commissioner McKay, and then was taken back to the penitentiary because he was not "allowed to take the oath required in order to avoid paying fine and cost of suit." "After a hearing before Judge Zane, in the Third District Court, on a writ of *habeas corpus*, Goff was released from imprisonment, by paying his fine."[139] Hyrum Goff died November 24, 1914, in Midvale, Utah.[140]

Maria T. Arnold Goff was born May 1, 1855, to Josiah Arnold and Clarissa L. Jones. Maria married Hyrum Goff as his first wife on January 2, 1871.[141] Maria had six sons and six daughters, four of whom died in their early childhood.[142] Their family lived in West Jordan, Utah.[143] Maria died May 3, 1932, in Midvale, Utah.[144]

Marinda P. Bateman Goff was born September 29, 1861, in West Jordan, Utah, to parents Samuel Bateman and Marinda Allen. She married Hyrum Goff as a plural wife on October 24, 1878, in Salt Lake City, and they resided in West Jordan, Utah.[145] They were the parents of three sons and five daughters.[146] Marinda Goff died in West Jordan on October 5, 1902.[147]

---

137. Jenson, *Church Chronology*, 127.
138. Jenson, *Church Chronology*, 129–30.
139. Jenson, *Church Chronology*, 136.
140. "Hyrum Goff Is Called by Death," *Deseret Evening News*, November 25, 1914, 2.
141. Esshom, *Pioneers and Prominent Men*, 893.
142. Jenson, *LDS Biographical Encyclopedia*, 309.
143. Esshom, *Pioneers and Prominent Men*, 893.
144. "Maria T. Goff Resident of Midvale Dies after Brief Illness," *Deseret Evening News*, May 4, 1932, 3.
145. Esshom, *Pioneers and Prominent Men*, 803.
146. Jenson, *LDS Biographical Encyclopedia*, 308–9.
147. "Death of Mrs. Goff: Estimable West Jordan Woman Passes to the Great Beyond," *Deseret Evening News*, October 6, 1902, 1.

John Wesley Greenman was born about 1840 in Ohio.[148] Greenman married Ann about 1866. The family lived in Wisconsin before moving to Utah. Once in Utah, Greenman worked as a Deputy U.S. Marshal in Salt Lake City.[149] Greenman had close surveillance of the Mormon prisoners who were serving time in the Utah Penitentiary for unlawful cohabitation.[150] Captain Greenman died at Oregon State Soldiers' home at Roseburg, Oregon, on April 1, 1917.[151]

Catherine (or Katherine, Kathryn) Houtz Groesbeck was born October 6, 1862, in Springville, Utah, to parents Jacob Houtz and Bridget Dailey.[152] She became the third wife of Nicholas H. Groesbeck on July 21, 1882, in Salt Lake City. They had four children, two boys and two girls.[153] She later married Mathias Erick Wahlin on September 11, 1901.[154] She died October 28, 1929, in Springville, Utah.[155]

Nicholas Harmon Groesbeck was born April 27, 1842, in Springfield, Sangamon, Illinois, to parents Nicholas Groesbeck and Elizabeth Thompson.[156] He came to Utah with his family on October 2, 1856.[157] He married three times: Rhoda Sanderson December 16, 1862, in Springville, Utah; Cornelia Melissa Sanford June 28, 1869, in Salt Lake City; and Katheryn Houtz

---

148. United States 1880 Federal Census, Salt Lake County, Utah, ED# 52, 37, lines 43–50.
149. 1880 Federal Census, 37.
150. Jenson, *Church Chronology*, 144.
151. "G. A. R. Comrades Die," *Deseret Evening News*, April 17, 1917, 7.
152. "Aged Woman Answers Call," *Provo Evening Herald*, October 28, 1929, 2; Esshom, *Pioneers and Prominent Men*, 902.
153. Esshom, *Pioneers and Prominent Men*, 902.
154. Ancestral File.
155. "Aged Woman Answers Call," 2.
156. Ancestral File.
157. Esshom, *Pioneers and Prominent Men*, 902.

July 27, 1882.[158] In 1871 he served a mission to Kentucky, Ohio, and Illinois. Nicholas died Mar 29, 1923, in Springville, Utah.[159]

Rhoda Rebecca Groesbeck was born November 16, 1868, in Springville, Utah, to Nicholas H. Groesbeck and Rhoda Sanderson. Rhoda married H. M. "Mack" Dougall in Springville in 1891.[160] Rhoda died October 2, 1956, in Springville, Utah.[161]

Jens Hansen was born March 15, 1837, in Gjerslev, Holbæk, Denmark, to parents Hans Jensen and Margrete Christensen. He married Bertha Jorgensen March 24, 1862, in Copenhagen, Denmark, and he married Kirsten Henricksen June 4, 1864, in Salt Lake City.[162] In 1881 he was called on a mission to Nebraska. He spent one year there and then transferred to the Scandinavian mission.[163] He served as second counselor in the Mill Creek Ward. On April 9, 1886, he was arrested on charges of unlawful cohabitation and sentenced June 2 with a $300 fine.[164] He was released December 2, 1886, but was arrested again April 27, 1888.[165] Jens Hansen died September 10, 1917, from being struck by an automobile on September 7, 1917.[166]

Ephraim Jensen was born in Brigham City, Utah, November 4, 1857, the son of Hans Peter Jensen and Sarah Clausen. In 1882 he filled a mission to the northern states, and on May 1, 1884, he married Hattie Critchlow. They were the parents of five sons and three

158. Ancestral File.
159. "Pioneer Mining Man Buried at Springville," *Deseret Evening News*, April 3, 1923, 3.
160. Esshom, *Pioneers and Prominent Men*, 902.
161. Obituary of Rhoda R. G. Dougall, *Deseret News and Telegram*, October 3, 1956, B12.
162. Ancestral File.
163. "Jens Hansen Dead as Result of Auto Accident," *Deseret Evening News*, September 11, 1917, 10.
164. Stan Larson, ed., *Prisoner for Polygamy: The Memoirs and Letters of Rudger Clawson at the Utah Territorial Penitentiary, 1884–1887* (Chicago: University of Illinois, 1993), 219; Jenson, *Church Chronology*, 133, 141.
165. Jenson, *Church Chronology*, 161.
166. "Jens Hansen Dead," 10.

daughters. In 1889 he became sheriff and justice of the peace in Brigham City. He served in the superintendency of the Logan Fifth Ward Sunday School. He served a mission to the eastern states in 1898 and then was called by President Lorenzo Snow to be the custodian of the Tabernacle grounds, and under the direction of the President, he established the Bureau of Information. He died October 24, 1939, in Salt Lake City.[167]

Hattie Critchlow Jensen was born January 31, 1864, in Riverdale, Utah, a daughter of William F. Critchlow and Mary Eliza Brown. She was married to Ephraim Jensen May 1, 1886. She served as Relief Society president of the Ocean Park branch in California and was appointed to a committee which prepared outlines of study for the Salt Lake Stake Relief Society. She was a member of the first women's committee of the Utah Genealogical Society, the Daughters of the Utah Pioneers, and Daughters of the Mormon Battalion. She died April 4, 1848, in Salt Lake City.[168]

Edna Leone Snow Lambert was born November 27, 1871, in Manti, Utah, to parents Gardner Elisha Snow and Esther Phelena Cox. She married Angus M. Lambert on February 11, 1891, in Manti, Utah. She served in the Relief Society organization and was a member of the Daughters of the Utah Pioneers. Mrs. Lambert died May 22, 1957, in Cedar City, Utah.[169]

Mary Alice Lambert was born August 10, 1878, to parents George C. Lambert and Mary Alice Needham.[170] She married

167. "Worker in Church Dies," *Deseret News*, October 25, 1939, 20.
168. "Active Church Worker of S. L. Dies," *Deseret News*, April 5, 1948, 19.
169. "Edna L. S. Lambert, Church Worker, Dies in Cedar City," *Deseret News*, May 23, 1957, D7; Ancestral File.
170. Esshom, *Pioneers and Prominent Men*, 994.

John Gray Peart on November 24, 1898, in Salt Lake City.[171] Her husband married twice more in 1893 and 1901. She was a member of the Mormon Tabernacle Choir. She died July 21, 1899, in Salt Lake City.[172]

Lillian Fannie (or Fanny Lillian) Loveland was born September 1, 1871, in Brigham City, Utah, to parents Chester Carlos Loveland and Mary Ann Barnes.[173] She was married first to Alviras Snow January 30, 1889, in Logan, Utah.[174] There must have been a divorce, because she was married a second time to Karl Emil Maeser, the son of Karl G. Maeser and Anna Henrietta Theresa Mieth, on March 29, 1894, in Logan, Utah, and Alviras Snow left Utah and was living in Kansas City, Missouri, before 1935. There are no known children of the first marriage, but she had four children with her second husband.[175] Lillian died September 13, 1939, in Upland, California.[176]

Clarissa Snow McAllister was born July 19, 1854, in Salt Lake City to parents Lorenzo Snow and Caroline Horton.[177] She married John Archibald McAllister on June 12, 1871, in Salt Lake City.[178] She died October 15, 1917, at Fort Douglas, Utah.[179]

Henry W. Naisbitt was born November 7, 1826, in North Allerton, England, to John Naisbitt and Martha Neede. Naisbitt joined the Church in 1850 and emigrated to the United States in 1854.[180]

171. "Death's Sorrowful Work: Alice Lambert Peart Passes from This Mortal Sphere," *Deseret News*, July 22, 1899, 8; marriage certificate, Salt Lake County, Book 1, #7892; Esshom, *Pioneers and Prominent Men*, 994.
172. "Death's Sorrowful Work," 8.
173. Ancestral File.
174. Marriage certificate of Alviras Snow and Lillian Fannie Loveland.
175. Ancestral File.
176. Ancestral File.
177. Esshom, *Pioneers and Prominent Men*, 1173; Ancestral File.
178. Ancestral File; Esshom, *Pioneers and Prominent Men*, 1173.
179. "Mrs. M'Allister Dies after Brief Illness," *Deseret Evening News*, October 15, 1917, 14.
180. Jenson, *LDS Biographical Encyclopedia*, 175.

He married Elizabeth Paul December 24, 1853.[181] After coming to Utah he also married four other women: Mary Ann Luff in October 1862; Catherine Hagell on April 13, 1867; Elizabeth Irvine on April 13, 1870; and Frances Hurst in 1879.[182] Naisbitt also contributed many hymns to both the LDS general and Sunday School hymnbooks.[183] Naisbitt was arrested on the charge of unlawful cohabitation March 19, 1886.[184] He was convicted of unlawful cohabitation on April 30, 1886, and on May 11, 1886, was sentenced to six months in prison and a $300 fine.[185] Naisbitt was discharged from the Utah Penitentiary November 11, 1886.[186] On February 3, 1890, Naisbitt was arrested a second time on the charge of unlawful cohabitation.[187] He was sentenced to six months in prison and taken to the penitentiary on May 12, 1890.[188] He was released from the penitentiary October 12, 1890,[189] and he died February 26, 1908.[190]

William Francis Olson was born May 26, 1869, in Fillmore, Utah, to parents George Daniel Olson and Delilah Cornelia King. He married Annie May Cluff November 27, 1895, in Salt Lake City. They were the parents of four children. He was set apart May 1, 1896, by J. Golden Kimball to serve a mission in Switzerland and Germany and returned August 20, 1898. He served as president of the YMMIA, teacher in Summit Stake Academy, mayor of Price (two terms), and organizer and vice president of Price Commercial and Savings Bank. He was married a second time

181. Ruth J. Martin, *Twentieth Ward History, 1856–1979* (n.p., 1979), 36.
182. Jenson, *LDS Biographical Encyclopedia*, 176.
183. Martin, *Twentieth Ward History*, 37.
184. Jenson, *Church Chronology*, 130.
185. Jenson, *Church Chronology*, 132.
186. Jenson, *Church Chronology*, 140.
187. Jenson, *Church Chronology*, 181.
188. Jenson, *Church Chronology*, 184.
189. Jenson, *Church Chronology*, 188.
190. Martin, *Twentieth Ward History*, 37.

to Daphne Dalton on July 24, 1928. William died January 12, 1953, in Long Beach, California.

Lydia Snow Pierce was born January 21, 1860, in Salt Lake City to parents Lorenzo Snow and Mary Elizabeth Houtz.[191] Lydia married Eli Harvey Pierce. They were the parents of four daughters. She was a YLMIA worker and a teacher at the University of Utah. Mrs. Pierce died December 22, 1898.[192]

George Lewis Savage was born January 27, 1865, in Salt Lake City to parents Charles Roscoe Savage and Annie Fenn Adkin. He married Lana Snow February 22, 1888, in Salt Lake City.[193] They were the parents of Geneva Savage, born July 12, 1892, in Salt Lake City.[194] George Lewis Savage died March 8, 1936, in Salt Lake City.[195]

Eliza R. Snow was born January 21, 1804, in Becket, Berkshire, Massachusetts, daughter of Oliver Snow and Rosetta L. Pettibone and sister of Lorenzo Snow.[196] She was baptized April 5, 1835.[197] She was sealed to the Prophet Joseph Smith June 29, 1842.[198] Eliza wrote many poems and hymns.[199] She died December 5, 1887, at the Lion House in Salt Lake City.[200]

191. Esshom, *Pioneers and Prominent Men*, 1173.
192. "Sudden Death of Mrs. Pierce," *Deseret News*, December 22, 1898, 2.
193. Ancestral File.
194. "Pioneer Utah Art Dealer Dies; Funeral Tuesday," *Deseret Evening News*, March 9, 1936, 3; Victor Grant Hillard Jr., *Descendants of John Hiller of Hadley, MA:* http://worldconnect.genealogy.rootsweb.com/cgi-bin/igm.cgi?op=GET&db=hadley&id=I1185.
195. "Pioneer Utah," 3.
196. Andrew Jenson, *LDS Biographical Encyclopedia*, 1:693–97.
197. Jenson, *LDS Biographical Encyclopedia*, 1:693–97.
198. Jenson, *LDS Biographical Encyclopedia*, 1:693–97.
199. Jenson, *LDS Biographical Encyclopedia*, 1:693–97.
200. Jenson, *LDS Biographical Encyclopedia*, 1:693–97.

Lana Snow was born October 22, 1863, in Brigham City, Utah, to parents Lorenzo Snow and Eleanor Houtz. Lana "spent her childhood in Brigham City" and "was a member of the Christian Science Church."[201] She married George Lewis Savage February 22, 1888, in Salt Lake City.[202] They were the parents of Geneva Savage, born July 12, 1892, in Salt Lake City.[203] Lana Snow Savage died July 16, 1951, in Salt Lake City.[204]

Alviras E. (or Laurin Alviras) Snow was born December 2, 1863, to parents Lorenzo Snow and Sarah Ann Prichard.[205] He graduated from the University of Utah in the fall of 1882.[206] He married Fanny Lillian Loveland on January 30, 1889, in Logan, Utah.[207] Following his release from prison, Lorenzo Snow was accompanied by Alviras in his carriage.[208] He studied law at Columbian University in Washington DC and graduated in 1897.[209]

LeRoi Clarence Snow was born August 26, 1876, in Brigham City, Utah, to parents Lorenzo Snow and Minnie Jensen.[210] He served in many Church positions, including librarian in the Salt Lake Temple, missionary in Germany from 1896 to 1899,[211] and chief tithing clerk. He also served as secretary to the president of the Eastern States Mission in 1921 and in 1922 was called as

201. "Mrs. Savage, Daughter of Pres. Snow, Dies," *Deseret News*, July 18, 1951, A5.
202. Ancestral File.
203. "Pioneer Utah Art Dealer Dies," *Deseret News*, 3; Hillard, *Descendants of John Hiller*: http://worldconnect.genealogy.rootsweb.com/cgi-bin/igm.cgi?op=GET&db=hadley&id=I1185, accessed March 17, 2001.
204. "Mrs. Savage, Daughter," *Deseret News*, A5.
205. Esshom, *Pioneers and Prominent Men*, 1173.
206. *Biographical Record of Salt Lake City and Vicinity: Containing Biographies of Well Known Citizens of the Past and Present* (Chicago: National Historical Record Company, 1902), 254.
207. Box Elder County marriages, Book 1, page 38.
208. Thomas C. Romney, *The Life of Lorenzo Snow, Fifth President of the Church of Jesus Christ of Latter-day Saints* (Salt Lake City: Sugarhouse Press, 1955), 365.
209. Romney, *Life of Lorenzo Snow*, 365.
210. Esshom, *Pioneers and Prominent Men*, 1173; Ancestral File.
211. Jenson, *LDS Biographical Encyclopedia*, 716.

president of the mission home in Salt Lake City until 1926.[212] He married Maud Mary Ford June 29, 1900, in Salt Lake City. They had one child.[213] He married Burma Celia Thompsonn on May 10, 1912, in Thatcher, Arizona, and they had three children.[214] LeRoi Snow died December 31 in Salt Lake City.[215]

Lorenzo Lamont Snow was born in Brigham City, Utah, on August 26, 1884. He was the youngest son of President Lorenzo Snow and Minnie Jensen. Snow was a navy captain and retired in Hartford, Connecticut, where he died on May 7, 1954.[216]

Minnie Mabelle Snow was born May 23, 1879, in Brigham City, Utah, to parents Minnie Jensen and Lorenzo Snow.[217] She married Alfred L. Cook of Logan, Utah, on February 10, 1904, in Salt Lake City.[218] She died December 3, 1962.[219]

Minnie Jensen Snow was born October 10, 1854, in Brigham City, Utah, to parents J. P. Jensen and Sarah Clawson.[220] She married Lorenzo Snow June 12, 1871, in Salt Lake City.[221] They were the parents of five children. She was a member of the general board of the YLMIA and was sent three times as a delegate to

212. "LeRoi C. Snow, Mission Home Ex-Leader, Dies," *Deseret News and Telegram*, January 1, 1963, 18B.
213. Jenson, *LDS Biographical Encyclopedia*, 716; Salt Lake County Marriage Licenses, Book J, #9372.
214. Jenson, *LDS Biographical Encyclopedia*, 716; "LeRoi C. Snow Dies," *Deseret News*, 18B.
215. "LeRoi C. Snow Dies," 18B.
216. "Lorenzo L. Snow, Son of Church President, Dies," *Deseret News and Telegram*, May 8, 1954, B5; Ancestral File.
217. Mabelle Snow entry, FHL film number 884079-884081; IGI v5.0, The Church of Jesus Christ of Latter-day Saints at Family Search, http://www.familysearch.com; original source, "Deceased membership records 1941–1988," The Church of Jesus Christ of Latter-day Saints. See also "Early Church Information File," FHL film number 1750715, The Church of Jesus Christ of Latter-day Saints, entries for Minnie Mabel Snow and Minne Mabelle Snow.
218. Salt Lake County Marriage Licenses, Book O, no. 14057.
219. Ancestral File.
220. Esshom, *Pioneers and Prominent Men*, 5.
221. Ancestral File.

the National Council of Women.[222] Minnie Jensen Snow died January 2, 1908.[223]

Willard Lycurgus Snow was born March 1842 in Lee County, Iowa, the son of Willard Snow and Melvina Harvey.[224] He married Sarah Ann Bower April 15, 1865,[225] and later married Flora Lewis Mousely on April 13, 1874.[226] Between his two wives, he was father to nineteen children.[227] He was a Black Hawk Indian War veteran, having served in John R. Winder's company.[228] He served as superintendent of the Farmers Ward Sunday School and as a member of the bishopric in Draper. He died February 1, 1920, in Forest Dale, Utah.[229]

Samuel Linzey (or Lindsay) Sprague was born March 22 or 23, 1843, in Lowell, Norfolk, Massachusetts, or Salem, Essex, Massachusetts to parents Dr. S. L. Sprague and Mary Woodard.[230] He married Anna Marian Kimball in 1868. He was a deputy United States Marshall 1871–1890 and was employed as a guard at the Utah Penitentiary.[231] On February 11, 1887, he made a raid on Church buildings with marshal Frank Dyer, John Greenman, and others. They were looking for John Taylor and George Q. Cannon, but did not find them.[232] Samuel L. Sprague died May 11, 1900.[233]

222. Jenson, *LDS Biographical Encyclopedia*, 5.
223. "Death of Mrs. Minnie J. Snow," *Deseret Evening News*, 5.
224. Esshom, *Pioneers and Prominent Men*, 101, 1174.
225. "Utah Pioneer of 1847 Is Buried at Draper," *Deseret Evening News*, February 14, 1920, 7.
226. Esshom, *Pioneers and Prominent Men*, 101, 1174.
227. Jenson, *LDS Biographical Encyclopedia*, 574.
228. Esshom, *Pioneers and Prominent Men*, 101, 1174; "Utah Pioneer," 7.
229. "Utah Pioneer," 7.
230. "Samuel L. Sprague Dead," *Deseret Evening News*, May 12, 1900, 1; Susan Easton Black, comp., *Membership of The Church of Jesus Christ of Latter-day Saints, 1830–1848* (Provo, UT: Religious Studies Center, Brigham Young University, 1989), 41:38; Esshom, *Pioneers and Prominent Men*, 1179.
231. Esshom, *Pioneers and Prominent Men*, 1179.
232. Jenson, *Church Chronology*, 144.
233. "Samuel L. Sprague Dead," 1; Jenson, *Church Chronology*, 4; Esshom, *Pioneers and Prominent Men*, 1179.

Elmina Shepard Taylor was born September 12, 1830, in Middle-field, Otsego, New York, to parents David Spaulding Shepard and Rosella Bailey. She married George Hamilton Taylor on August 31, 1856, in Haverstraw, Rockland, New York. George later married two other wives in Utah in 1877 and 1885. Elmina and George were the parents of seven children.[234] Elmina was the president of the YLMIA from 1880 to 1904.[235] She died December 6, 1904, in Salt Lake City.[236]

Stanley Taylor was born February 4, 1838, in Bolton, Lancashire, England, to parents William Taylor and Ann Jones. He married Hannah Howard on May 6, 1863, in Salt Lake City. They were the parents of eight children.[237] He married second wife Mary Ann Howard on February 3, 1866, and they had eleven children. He was convicted on April 26, 1886, of unlawful cohabitation and sentenced May 10 to the "full penalty of the law—six months' imprisonment, a fine of $300 and cost of suit."[238] He died August 13, 1921, in Salt Lake City.[239]

Charles Schuster Zane was born March 21, 1831, in Tuckahoe, Cumberland, New Jersey, to parents Andrew Zane and Mary Franklin. He was educated at McKendry College in Illinois. Judge Zane was the first chief justice of the State of Utah. During his tenure hundreds of people were convicted of illegal cohabitation or polygamy. He died March 29, 1915, in Salt Lake City.[240]

---

234. Ancestral File; Esshom, *Pioneers and Prominent Men*, 1201; Jenson, *LDS Biographical Encyclopedia*, 267.
235. Jenson, *LDS Biographical Encyclopedia*, 267.
236. Ancestral File; "Young Ladies' President Dead," *Deseret Evening News*, November 6, 1904, 1.
237. Ancestral File; Carter, *Our Pioneer Heritage*, 178–200.
238. Carter, *Our Pioneer Heritage*, 178–200.
239. "Last Call Comes to Early Settler of Utah," *Deseret News*, August 15, 1921, 6.
240. "Judge Charles S. Zane Called Suddenly by Death," *Deseret Evening News*, March 20, 1915, 14.

Index